TRICKS JOURNALISTS PLAY

Dennis Barker is an experienced journalist who has worked for *The Guardian* in many different roles, from reporter, feature writer and media correspondent to columnist, since the 1960s, and at the moment is a contributor of obituaries, mainly in the media and entertainment spheres. He is the author of many books, including *The Craft of the Media Interview, How to Deal with the Media: a Practical Guide*, the People of the Forces trilogy: *Soldiering On, Ruling the Waves* and *Guarding the Skies, One Man's Estate* and three novels. He also broadcast regularly with the BBC in the 1970s.

Also by Dennis Barker

Non-fiction

The Craft of the Media Interview
How to Deal with the Media
Soldiering On
Ruling the Waves
Guarding the Skies
One Man's Estate
Parian Ware
Fresh Start

Novels

Candidate of Promise
The Scandalisers
Winston Three Three Three

Tricks Journalists Play

HOW THE TRUTH
IS MASSAGED, DISTORTED,
GLAMORIZED AND GLOSSED OVER

by

Dennis Barker

dlm

First published in 2007
by Giles de la Mare Publishers Limited
53 Dartmouth Park Hill, London NW5 1JD

Typeset by Tom Knott
Printed by Cromwell Press Ltd
Trowbridge, Wiltshire

Dennis Barker is hereby identified as author of
this work in accordance with Section 77 of the
Copyright, Designs and Patents Act 1988

A CIP record of this book is available
from the British Library

ISBN 9781900357272 paperback original

Contents

Acknowledgements

My thanks to all those whose work has contributed to the points in this book, and to Giles de la Mare for his constant interest and encouragement, and his editing of it.

My thanks also to my wife Sarah for her superior mastery of the computer and to our daughter Ellie for tolerating her father's preoccupation with the keyboard.

Introduction

Whenever in recent years there has been a national opinion poll on the public's esteem for, and trust of, people in various professions, nurses have come somewhere near the top, while estate agents, politicians and journalists have come near the bottom.

Estate agents and politicians may be predictably unpopular: both have a vested interest in *selling* something to the public, whether it is a property or a policy. But *journalists?* They should surely be the friends and champions of the public, not the objects of its distrust and contempt. The placing of them near the bottom of the list is nothing less than a gathering disaster, not only for the journalists themselves, but for the politicians and other public figures they deal with, and for society as a whole.

The affair of the BBC journalist Andrew Gilligan and his widely believed – then and since – allegation that the government had 'sexed up' the intelligence services' information on the possibility of weapons of mass destruction being launched from Iraq at forty-five minutes' notice, as a preliminary to its helping in the invasion of Iraq, undoubtedly increased public interest in the rights and wrongs of journalistic practices, sometimes in relation to the rights and wrongs of the practices of spin-doctors. In the Gilligan case, the Hutton inquiry criticized the BBC, and its Director-General Greg Dyke resigned. But as far as the government's role was concerned, the report of the inquiry was widely thought to be a 'whitewash'.

Of course journalists have tricks of the trade. But they are not always wrong in their techniques and judgments, especially when they try to counter official 'spin'. However, if, as can happen, they merely try to replace official spin with their own spin, that can be unhelpful to the people who really matter: the public. Campaigns of denigration of people in the public eye, especially though not exclusively politicians, can alienate the public who are supposedly 'protected' by press freedom. This can certainly happen if the attacks suggest less a search for truth than a modern version of bear-baiting, cock-fighting or any other activity pandering to those who simply like the sight, not of truth, but of blood.

Today it might provoke cynical smiles or even outright laughter if someone should claim that, at its best, journalism is one of the most vital and valuable vocations. I do not think such cynical smiles would have been produced when I entered journalism over half a century ago. Some may try to dismiss this by saying, 'Oh, come on; times have changed!' Times have indeed changed. They are always changing. But a truth is still a truth, a lie is still a lie, and a distortion is still a distortion, and will be for ever more. Honestly telling people at one end of the street what is going on at the other, which is the essence of journalism, is invaluable, and indeed indispensable. Without it, democratic votes would be next to worthless because there would be no adequate information on which any voter could take a wise and well-informed decision.

If journalism is not essentially about being the friend of honesty, the friend of the people and the critic of the misbehaving rich and powerful, if people do not trust it as a friend of their hopes and their rights, ultimately it is nothing but spin-assisted and spin-assisting fantasy, handout re-writing, knee-jerk denigration, money-making and self-aggrandisement.

The essence of good journalism is to avoid tricks and 'tell it as it is', without editorializing and sensationalizing, in news columns as distinct from leading articles and leader-page articles. At the present time, there are two powerful pressures against 'telling it as it is', and for adopting trickery.

The first is commercial. In the 1970s, and more so in the Thatcher years of the 1980s, the managers of newspapers started referring to journalism as 'product'. It was a revealing and disquieting term. Their stated aim was to have a better 'product' than that of their rivals for the reader to consume. This is the language of the barrow boy rather than the journalist. Journalism is not a product like butter or sausages. It is a *service*: a difficult concept to get to grips with in an era when the whole concept of service in any shape or form, and its importance to tolerable living, has been overrun by the search for profits – money having become virtually the sole measurement of personal status and skill in a money-obsessed civilization.

Those in print journalism who make judgments in terms of 'product' and money-generation *alone* were up against the fact that television and radio were now the dominant means of supplying hard news to the public. They came to the conclusion that souped-up news, or comment pieces on issues the public already knew about (in the past the ingredients of magazines rather than newspapers), were the best means of continuing to sell newspapers. Newspapers became more strident in their competition with television, and television started counter-attacking in stridency, both media becoming rather like speeding Titanics heading for an iceberg.

That iceberg was the public's low opinion of journalists, as repeatedly expressed in those opinion polls.

The second pressure against 'telling it as it is' is the glamour and celebrity status of *some* journalists, who were to become rivals or opponents of the people they were writing about, rather than honest observers. Today we have, on the one hand, indulged and well-paid journalistic 'stars', who are usually pontificators rather than on-the-spot reporters, and on the other, perhaps anonymous, under-paid and under-regarded craftsmen who do the routine (some would say the 'real') work. The old-fashioned newspaper reporter had his notebook and his pen, but he rarely had glamour or celebrity to tempt him into producing 'performance' journalism.

The television journalist talking straight to camera is a rather different case. He may perhaps be excused for being *self*-conscious, especially if reporting from any sort of battlefront, where his self can become a legitimate litmus paper for detecting what is going on and for conveying a decent feeling about it. In the television *studio*, however, with narcissism not instilling the same discipline and restraint as outside circumstances, trickiness can intervene. Interviews of politicians and others can begin to take on the appearance of battles for supremacy between two equals rather than a search for information and enlightenment. Whether the interview is with the Prime Minister, the Archbishop of Canterbury or a distinguished scientist, it can on occasion seem as if a *victory* for the journalist interviewer has to be chalked up. This form of 'telling it as it is' means telling it as the executives behind the studio interviewer see it, or telling it as the interviewer's vanity sees it, even if the result is without great benefit to people listening or watching.

Combative television and radio journalists can and sometimes do claim that displaying pugnacity is a trick which is justified because it produces truths. If there has ever been a case of a government minister in such an interview collapsing and saying, 'Boo-hoo! I've been rumbled! I can't go on! I must confess everything!' I am afraid I have not witnessed it nor heard of it. Virtuoso journalists employing this sort of trick usually succeed only in turning politicians and others into more plausible and efficient liars. That can be to the detriment of the public rather than to its advantage.

Does this analysis mean that whoever accepts it wants journalists to 'go easy' on celebrities? Not at all. Pugnacious and destructive interviewing by journalists tends to make those questioned close up rather than open out. A conversation between one human being and another is arguably more likely to reveal something of value. And tricks in the presentation of news, especially in the distortion of news in order to produce blooded drama not necessarily justified by the cold facts, will make celebrities of any sort close up even more in the future.

If the public is not necessarily informed by narcissistic tricks, is it at least impressed? Once again, the answer is the presence of journalism towards the bottom of the list of respected occupations.

Real journalism, as distinct from attention-seeking, wrestling-match entertainment to fill in the spaces between lucrative advertisements, consists of a reporter finding and filing as many facts and sincere impressions as possible from the scene of whatever is the action. It might be argued that instead we too often have propaganda based on the spoon-feeding of spin-doctors; tabloid soap-opera fashioned around clichéd and often insignificant characters who may be actors, singers, footballers, politicians or serial killers; crude or exotic smut tailored for those with nothing better to think about; the opinionated droolings onto word-processor screens which ultimately fill a multitude of armchair columnists' slots (whereas most newspapers used to make do with a single serious columnist such as the late great Sir William Connor, Cassandra of the *Daily*

Mirror); public-relations sycophancy served up in agreed text and pictures for money, in glossily vacuous fan-magazines; and sour and obsessive destructiveness masquerading as social concern and criticism.

That great American pundit Walter Lippmann talked of good journalism as 'a picture of reality on which citizens can act'. Is this what we have now? Or is journalism lurching into a repertoire of money-making tricks and tricksiness? That last question is of great concern to all readers, listeners and viewers. If the answer to it were ever to be 'yes', it would imply the coarsening of public debate and private expectations, the distortion of the basis of political and moral judgments and the corruption of our view of our fellow human beings.

In recent years there have been a number of criticisms of contemporary journalism, but they have all seemingly passed by with no result. Why has no organization or individual outside journalism campaigned consistently for a re-think within journalism? Primarily, one suspects, because they fear turning the powerful media into an enemy. Thus the media have been encouraged to feel that any criticism of them can be merely brushed aside, and need not be taken seriously. If this is so, it ironically *threatens* press and broadcasting freedom. It gives ammunition to any government wanting to impose statutory controls on the media, safe in the knowledge that the public are as much disillusioned with journalists as with politicians, or more so.

But the brushing off of criticism from outside as merely a self-serving attack by Authority, Eminence or Celebrity, implies that any reappraisal of contemporary journalism does have to come from *within*, the public having already declared themselves in the opinion polls. This is why, in *defence* of a craft I have practised for sixty years, and have regarded as one of the most necessary jobs there is, I have tried to point out some of the ways in which journalism is in danger of alienating the public whose helpful friend any self-respecting journalist should hope to be. One trusts that human intelligence within the job will bring about some measure of voluntary reform.

If I have an increasingly frequent daytime nightmare, it is of a future government seeking to impose statutory controls on journalism, *and the public who are supposed to be protected by journalists' freedom being strongly in favour of government controls over a distrusted occupation.*

It would be helpful if, while we are waiting for intelligence within journalism to begin to function on this issue, the public could recognize, and if necessary discount, some of the increasingly common tricks. Some are major, some are minor – little more than irritations. But even the irritations can subliminally cause journalists *not* to be valued and trusted. I have described here a range of journalistic tricks of all shapes and sizes, and of varying degrees of importance, all of which may in their own way cause the public to think less of journalism and journalists.

A Revealing Battle

Mutual mistrust at fever pitch, especially if both parties suspect conscious trickery, is difficult to live with constructively. The recent long-drawn-out conflict between the media and the beleaguered Deputy Prime Minister John Prescott disclosed a lot about the contemporary attitudes and tricks of both public figures and journalists.

On 6 July 2006, after intense interest from journalists in his affair with his diary secretary, and then his acceptance of hospitality from an American billionaire businessman wanting to run a gambling casino in the Dome south of the Thames, John Prescott was on the BBC Radio *Today* programme being questioned at length by the journalist John Humphrys. In the course of the interview, John Prescott accused the media of using a technique in attacking himself and politicians in general. He did not use the word 'trick' but that was the sense of what he was saying.

The trick, as he described it, was in essence this. A newspaper such as the *Daily Mail*, no friend of Labour governments, printed allegations, substantiated or not. Then other papers took them up and repeated them, and this went on until there was a grilling of the politician concerned on the *Today* programme, whatever substance there had or hadn't been in the original allegations. That made it difficult for a government minister to get on with his job, although he himself was determined to do so. The Deputy Prime Minister then launched into an explanation of what his job was in relation to the Dome, and in relation to other matters. He kept on talking, or trying to talk, about those while John Humphrys continually asked him, or tried to ask him, whether he had had other affairs than that with his diary secretary. Before the end, both the politician and the journalist were talking over one another.

No doubt listeners came to their own conclusions about this particular contest and the tricks being deployed, that were partly dependent on their political views, their notions of sexual morality and public responsibility, and their opinions on the role of journalists in holding politicians to account. What was undeniable was that it provided an illustration of tricks on both sides, notably that of keeping on talking whatever questions are being asked, or answers are being given.

John Humphrys is a professional of integrity, an exceptionally able questioner who has worked his way up through the hard slog of provincial journalism in his ungilded youth rather than living on a personal and professional Cloud Nine: quick-thinking, persistent and to the point, and equally tough towards both sides in a controversy.

But no questioning procedure exists in isolation. The ethos of the era in which it is being deployed will affect it, and at present that ethos includes talking down Deputy Prime Ministers or even Prime Ministers and arguing, rather than simply eliciting answers and letting the public decide. Taking the stance of a crusader against the interviewee's trickery could be, in hands more partisan than those of John Humphrys, a trick in itself.

John Prescott is a rugged personality in an era which is not short of supine placemen, a politician who once punched a hostile demonstrator who had thrown an egg into his face. His stance is that of a man who is eager to 'get on with the job in hand' (a prime virtue in the working classes from which his abilities extracted him) despite time-wasting interruptions. In his own job this meant, to him, getting the conversation back to government policy and mainstream political activities rather than indulging in personal tittle-tattle. While radiating businesslike candour, this sort of approach can also be a trick: at worst an attempt to kill a nasty smell by introducing Eau de Cologne rather than soap and water.

All the same, it would be a trick by an *elected* politician. Some people use the word 'democracy' in every other sentence without asking themselves whether it can or should mean treating democratically elected figures with respect. The fact of being elected now offers insubstantial protection to figures who would once have been treated seriously until they were actually caught with their hands in the till and found guilty.

The trick of *not* treating them seriously – for instance referring in headlines to Prescott as 'Two Jags' because he once had two Jaguar cars at his disposal – helps make politicians and other public figures into soap-opera characters. As such, and this is where journalists might reflect on the possible consequences of their own tricks, they may lose their jobs this week but be invited back next month or the month after to another job, as if nothing real had happened. Just another twist in the script. How exciting. Better than *EastEnders* or *Coronation Street*.

We have seen several examples of this process lately. Public figure 'shamed'. Public figure ejected from his job as unworthy. Then, public figure takes up another job, presumably now considered worthy. Logically, if you don't take office-holders seriously, you cannot take their actions and offences seriously, and there is no reason why they shouldn't go on offending for ever, coming back the following week, month or year as if nothing *real* had happened.

At one point in the interview with John Prescott, when John Humphrys sought to find out whether the Deputy Prime Minister had had other affairs, John Prescott said that the media didn't like him and, to be frank, he didn't like them either. A certain tension between the politicians and journalists is healthy, indeed necessary; but overall animosity and sourness is not healthy: it is mutually destructive. At another point in this revealing interview, John Prescott attempted to turn the tables by asking John Humphrys a personal question, which the journalist refused to answer on the grounds that he was not the Deputy Prime Minister. John Prescott said tartly that he was behaving as if he were.

And there, in essence, is a blueprint for journalist-public-figure relations at the present time: the journalist battles against the guile of public figures he tends to trust less and less; and the public figures resent the fact, as they see it, that journalists are increasingly giving themselves airs, regarding themselves as being on a par with those elected figures.

In examining politicians' tricks and journalists' tricks in such situations, as well as in others less conspicuous, the listener, or for that matter the newspaper reader, may well be tempted to ask: which came first, the chicken or the egg? The bludgeoning journalist out for blood, or the tricky politician who has almost certainly been on a media-training course?

To some extent the answer is irrelevant. We are where we are *now*. The question for journalists is: do contemporary tricks serve or offend the public? In some ways they do serve the public. Journalists' questions may at least reveal something about the interviewee's *character*, if not much more about the particular points at issue. And politicians' tricks for holding journalists at arm's length may perhaps be justified on the grounds that they enable affairs of state to proceed smoothly rather than sinking into muddle and anarchy.

Journalists who feel that their tricks, almost *any* tricks, are justified because they at least claim the listener's, the viewer's, or the reader's attention in apathetic times when milder methods might not, may overlook one salient possibility. The public may be hypnotized by tricks, and they may have a gory interest in the results – the hounding of ministers, and so on. But all the same, they may resent the trickster and have more human sympathy for the target of the trick than they would have in a more formal and polite age. An alcoholic may genuinely hate the barman, even though he is captured by the drink he serves. Is there a danger that the public may hate journalistic tricks, and that that is one of the reasons why journalists score so low in the polls?

Progress has been made in the electronic processes available to those who make an appearance in the electronic media, or write and present newspapers. There has been a great concentration of thought on the means of production. But progress may have a price. The numbers of underpaid journalists on local and regional newspapers who feel as if they are ill-paid peasants being pushed around merely to suit their employers' balance sheets, without reference to the needs of good journalism; the national newspapermen who find the apparently un-fettered prejudices of their proprietors difficult to take; and the magazine staff who are servants of the desire to make the bookstalls look glitzier – they may all indicate that too much attention is being given to technical means and too little to journalistic standards, since any transgressors will feel quite confident that all criticism can be swept aside as 'old-fashioned'.

The essential fact remains that progress in one direction can lead to deterioration in others; and that journalistic tricks, in small or larger degree, can influence what the public think not only about the people journalists are dealing with, but also about the journalists themselves as a professional class. The technological means now available to them may have improved their coverage in some respects. But arguably it is at a price.

2

The Price of Progress?

Many tricks currently played on the public through journalism must be laid at the door of editorial managers and the commercial managers above them rather than individual reporters. Such editorial policy can often be attributed to a panicky response to the fear of falling circulations or ratings. But what happens at the so-called 'coal-face' between journalists and the people they talk to can also have unfortunate effects.

They may seem an ill-assorted list but speculation, fact and notetaking can sometimes be dangerously bound together in a journalist's life. At the most simple level, in reporting a speaker who has said that some people think the government are shysters, it is fatally easy to report him as saying that *he* thinks the government are shysters – if the reporter has taken no accurate, clear and full shorthand note.

The sometimes almost unconscious trick of distortion may have been made easier by the difference in the 'props' used when a journalist meets people with whom he is going to talk. Until recent years, shorthand was regarded as absolutely necessary for any reporter, whether it was Pitman, Gregg or any of the speed-writing alternatives.

Progress, or 'progress', usually has a price. Shorthand is now dismissed as 'very yesterday'. Electronic devices are much more foolproof. And so on. But part of the price of electronic aids to the reporter has been a change in the stance of the reporter and therefore a change in his relationship with the people he is talking to. The dynamics of the confrontation have shifted. Electronics can produce tricks in that relationship which may not be altogether healthy.

At its most basic level, a microphone may be seen as in-trusive, even invasively threatening, in a way that a humble notebook and pen would not. And a television camera and film crew, by reinforcing group-think among journalists, may be more concerned with confirming pre-held views rather than finding out the facts. The member of the public or the celebrity being questioned may with reason have a sense of being out-numbered, out-gunned and at the mercy of someone else's group-think.

The mere existence of a microphone or recording machine, as distinct from a notebook, may condition what is said or not said; and readers, listeners and viewers would be wise to be aware of that fact when assessing what is reported and how.

One factor was not much commented on when the Mayor of London, Ken Livingstone, clashed with London *Evening Stan-dard* reporter Oliver Finegold, who tried to question him as he was leaving a South Bank party to celebrate the twentieth anniversary of the ex-minister Chris Smith's 'coming out' as a homosexual.

The Mayor was asked outside whether he had enjoyed the party – a perfectly proper question if it was not asked in a snide manner, which it was never suggested it had been. The Mayor responded by asking the reporter if he were a war criminal. When the reporter pointed out that he was Jewish and that he found the observation offensive, the Mayor replied: 'Well, you might be, but actually you are just like a concentration camp guard – you are just doing it because you are paid to, aren't you?' He went on in a similar vein, saying that those who worked for the paper were scumbags and that the organization owning it were fascists.

In subsequent days, then weeks, Livingstone refused to apologize, although urged to do so by Jewish organizations, by all the parties represented on the London Assembly and by the Prime Minister. Much was made of the fact that the reporter had the exchange on tape, so that it could not be denied. But it did not appear to occur to anyone that the fact that the Mayor was faced by a recorder rather than a notebook might itself have had an influence on his words and attitude, which in different circumstances he himself might have seen as being the sort of silly excess to which even intelligent people can descend on a fraught occasion.

It might be thought that the distinction between a notebook and a recorder in such circumstances is merely a quibble. It certainly might be thought so by anyone not familiar with the practice of reporting. But in fact the production of a recording machine, or, even more so, a television camera, can have its effects on an interviewee, just as the production of a notebook can – and the two sets of effects can be significantly different. All the people concerned, including readers, listeners or viewers of the outcome, should periodically remind themselves of this.

The London Mayor claimed that the recorder had been 'thrust' at him. This was his *perception* of what happened, whatever the truth may have been. Such a 'thrust' would have been practically an invitation to indiscretion and excess. It could be described as a sort of theatrical stage inviting the Mayor to *perform*, whereas a notebook could have been a signal that what was being taken down in notes had better be seriously thought out and defensible. Arguably, if the reporter had questioned the Mayor while bent over a notebook, the Mayor might never have allowed himself to make remarks which got him into deep and pointless trouble. Even if he had uttered them, he would have been more likely to have seen at once that the words were divorced from reality, as if he had accused someone forcing unwanted journalistic attentions on him of being Jack the Ripper. He might well have adroitly added: 'Look, I lost my patience with you, but I withdraw those remarks. You have been hanging around this event for hours, no doubt hoping for something compromising or unpleasant which would please your right-wing employers, and I suggest you now go home as I intend to do.'

Of course, in print journalism the reader may not be able to find out what form of aide-memoire was used. But journalists themselves know. A general principle might be that if you want a performance use a recorder; if you want the truth of a person's position and beliefs, use a notebook. If you want frothy nonsense, use a recorder; if you want facts and reasoned argument use a notebook. Politicians and public figures, as well as journalists, should be aware of the dangers.

Some might argue that it is not the business of journalists to, as it were, steady up the people they are talking to so that they do not commit indiscretions. At one level, this is certainly correct: if the man in the news is a criminal swindling elderly widows or a politician acting contrary to his professed beliefs, there is a case for using any means to get him to blurt out the truth. But in practice this rarely happens: crooks of all shapes and sizes know how to be glib in the most difficult conditions.

Clearly, some newspapers – not the *Evening Standard* – may actively want frothy nonsense rather than the truth because it can generate bigger and dafter headlines; but that position would be difficult to defend before any responsible jury, even in times when more and more media content is supposed to be entertainment rather than enlightenment. It is a mischievous trick which leads to a waste of time and to the debasing of reasonable argument into pointless name-calling. Journalism should surely assist in the enlightenment of the public, not its debauchery. A lot of the time, it does; some of the time, it does not.

In my book *The Craft of the Media Interview*, I mentioned some advantages of the notebook. In his review of it in *The Times*, Raymond Snoddy, then the capable and energetic media editor of that newspaper, argued reasonably but I hope pessimistically that the battle of the notebook versus electronic devices was already lost. But perhaps no battle is ever *permanently* lost, as the Germans may reflect as they enjoy their ownership of those great British creations, Rolls Royce, Bentley and Mini Cooper cars more than sixty years after losing the second world war.

Nor is it true to say: 'You can't turn back the clock.' We *do* turn back the clock, once every year when autumn arrives. One certainly can't reverse *time*, but man-made devices like clocks, recorders and notebooks (and for that matter Concorde and spaceships) can be intelligently adjusted to suit human needs, and can be used as and when human beings decide to use them, and be discarded or relegated to the sidelines when human beings decide. We may also remember how Coca Cola, after spending thousands if not millions of dollars, reversed its decision to introduce a new updated formula for its internationally famous drink when its customers showed that they preferred the original recipe. Concorde led the world. But Concorde was eventually withdrawn.

Some reporters, especially in one-to-one interviews or press conferences, now use electronic notebooks with keyboards for the immediate typing out of the gist of what is said. Is this a sound electronic trick? If a journalist types out a few bits and pieces on his electronic notebook, inevitably according to his preconceptions about what is important and what is not, is he likely to be less bound by facts and more open to speculation than if he had taken a full shorthand note and carefully read it afterwards? Psychologically, it can enable him to cut corners with an easier conscience than if he had a full and accurate note by his side. At the very least, he may fail to note possible qualifications to what his story claims; qualifications which may make a big difference.

Even accurate journalists may not be fully protected by the electronic notebook. When the gifted journalist central to the dispute over the terms on which Britain went to war in Iraq in 2003, whom we have already mentioned, Andrew Gilligan, then defence correspondent of the BBC Radio's *Today* programme, showed a BBC executive notes of his talk with the tragic weapons expert Dr David Kelly, who was later found dead, he said that all notes tended to be 'partial'. By this, of course, he plainly meant 'incomplete' rather than 'one-sided'.

This may be true in practice, but it might be better if it were not so. Veteran journalists might be tempted to tell all reporters, from those on local weeklies to serious national dailies, from those on local radio stations to national television news services, 'If you use an electronic notebook rather than old-fashioned shorthand, your notes may be very "partial" indeed. They may not be complete enough to save your deserved professional reputation, and the needs of truth, if your accurate story is disputed.'

After reading his own shorthand note, and seeing exactly what was said and what was not said, a journalist is less likely to open himself up to the accusation that he has accepted speculation as fact, or put his own interpretation onto what he has been told. It would be easier unconsciously to hype up brief notes taken on an electronic notebook than it would be to hype up a remark taken down in shorthand, for the simple reason that the writing of a substantial shorthand note on every important point requires so much concentration and dexterity of hand that it is not easy to re-interpret a statement about a possibility into becoming a statement about a probability, or a statement about a probability into becoming a statement about a certainty. Whatever a reporter may *want* to hear in such a situation, he will be restricted by his own note-taking.

Tape-recorders, undoubtedly useful in some circumstances, are not as invincibly fool-proof as is sometimes claimed. They can be compromised by two speakers simultaneously talking over one another, so that only a muddle of sound is to be heard afterwards rather than there being a watertight defence against any claim of inaccuracy.

Whether he uses shorthand or electronic means, a reporter may realize that he has missed some part of a statement, or is not sure of the accuracy of his note. What trick does he adopt in such circumstances? Perhaps he goes to ask another member of the press pack with whom he is on friendly terms if he can help. Although this can often be legitimate and useful in avoiding unnecessary errors, it can be less defensible when a press pack get together, share their notes and agree on what an important quote *was*.

Group-think is a trick with dangers. I once covered for *The Guardian* a press conference called by Scotland Yard at the height of the IRA terrorist offences in the 1970s. After the press conference, taxis were thin on the ground, so a large number of journalists, from tabloids and broadsheets, piled into the first passing taxi, which we directed towards Fleet Street. As the taxi pulled away, we started talking about what the government's response to the statements made by the police *could* be: a fair enough speculation. When we were half-way to our destination, the prediction of a possibility had turned into a probability; and by the time we had reached our destination, with me increasingly silent, the probability had become an established fact.

It was well before the days of mobile phones. No one in the taxi could have had any more actual information when they left the taxi than when they boarded it. It was of course quite possible that everyone had been talking principally for effect and that later everyone checked out the 'fact', and either substantiated it or abandoned it. This would make the speculation posing as fact in the taxi fair enough – with one proviso. It can be a dangerous thing for a journalist to go into a story having already made up his mind, or with his news-desk having made up his mind for him, about what the facts are. He may be professional enough to abandon suppositions if they do not check out. On the other hand, he may be a reporter who regards it as 'professional' to give those in authority or eminence an automatic bad time – that modern view of journalistic 'professionalism', which transforms a journalist from being a seeker after truth into a counsel for the prosecution. It is no more a good idea than transforming him into a counsel for the defence.

Every occupation has its cowboys and chancers. It would be strange if journalism didn't have any. Some cynics might argue that the more personally arrogant and self-important a journalist is, the more surely (at least for a time) he will climb the greasy pole to journalistic stardom.

But the greater will be the risk that he will confuse his or the news-desk's speculations with the facts, and his own wishes with the truth, until the time comes when he brings himself disastrously to his knees – as well as the cause of truth itself. Most transgressors whose twisting of facts runs ahead of their news-desks' or proprietors' wishes don't last for long.

A different professional development has had its impact on the ego rather than the truth-seeking skills of journalists, and is worth exploring.

3

The Death of the Reporter

By the 1970s, the national newspaper, radio or television general reporter was an endangered species, and by the 1980s readers and viewers might have thought that he (or she) had practically ceased to exist. The results deserve analysis and, more importantly, we should continually be aware of them.

General reporters have been increasingly replaced by specialist 'Correspondents' and 'Editors' who are supposed to be, and often are, experts in their own particular fields, not mere hacks whose job it is to go around asking the real experts simple and direct questions. Any personal by-line which does not have the benefit of a tag reading 'Northern Affairs Editor' (actually a reporter based in the northern branch office) or 'Home Affairs Correspondent' (practically any reporter not operating abroad) have come to look embarrassingly self-denigratory.

Dry smiles at elaborate titles are not unknown within the industry, but they are possibly not frequent enough. On 14 June 2006, the London *Evening Standard* reported that management consultants at the *Telegraph* group's Canary Wharf headquarters winced at the word 'reporters' and preferred to call such people 'information gatherers'. The fact is that the modern journalist tends to feel that he faces his colleagues naked if he does not bear a more important job description than the one-word 'reporter'.

Because such 'expert' and grandly-titled journalists spend all their time on a narrower range of stories than the general reporter has done, they do indeed inevitably acquire more knowledge of their subject. This often gives the people they are questioning a rougher ride, which can sometimes be a good thing.

But some of the psychological effects, as played out on the page and screen, are not. The change sometimes leads to the supposition by the specialist 'Correspondents' or 'Editors' that they are in fact better than mere journalists and as clever as, or even cleverer than, the people they are questioning – and that they are duty bound to demonstrate this supposed superiority to the public by creating and winning a battle not for truth but for supremacy. Instead of diligence and occasional self-mockery, they are expected to have what in other contexts is called Attitude.

The results are often visible. Especially in the political field, interviews sometimes become battles for supremacy between two almost equally self-important professionals, one the politician, the other the journalist, as we have seen. The public is ill-served when this happens, and should make sure it recognizes it when it does. It is too much to expect politicians to give up their self-importance – they are vain by temperament and have been elected by the public – but journalists tend to lose their hold on their public, as distinct from rival colleagues, when they acquire it.

Fortunately, it is not difficult to detect journalistic tricks that are designed, consciously or unconsciously, to inflate the reputation of the journalist rather than to serve the public. The most transparent trick is the one where the specialist Correspondent or Editor concentrates on a miniscule point of fact where the politician may be on shaky ground, and uses this as if it were an indication of the politician's overall political position or character.

The pseudo-school-examination question is a good example. It is a question on which the politician is likely to stumble, even though such an outcome has in fact little or no bearing on his competence in doing his job.

If politician A has just been made Education Secretary, he may be asked how many teachers there are in the country. The journalist, who may have been an Education Correspondent or even an Education Editor for years, and is himself aware of this statistic, has no need to ask the question, and the public will not gain much by its being asked. It is being asked purely to show the Correspondent or Editor in a good light and the politician in a bad one. If the politician hedges, he will appear shifty, and if he answers and is out by a few thousand, then the not so latent suggestion is that he is uninformed and unfit for his new job.

Or the specialist journalist may put a question in a joshing

manner which is supposed to prevent the man being interviewed from taking offence, but which nevertheless hides a
trap that cannot easily be side-stepped. A good example would
be when the new Education Secretary is asked in the broadcasting studio to perform a feat of mental arithmetic that a large
number of school pupils have been criticized for failing. Being
in a new job, in a broadcasting studio, in a press conference
and possibly in a funk, the minister is quite likely to give a
wrong answer or else no answer.

What in fact has happened here? The byline-enobled journalist has reinforced his own self-importance at the expense of the
politician's in a private battle for supremacy. The public has
been told nothing worth knowing, and the politician is encouraged to go on a media-training course that will make him a
more weasly and, in effect, more dishonest operator than he
need have been. And such questions are more likely to be asked
by a Political Editor or a Political Correspondent, or even a
Political Reporter, than by a mere general reporter.

As far as print journalism is concerned, there may be a
mischievous case for arguing that there is room for only one
'editor' on a newspaper, the rest of the out-of-the-office opera-
tives knowing themselves as reporters. Labour reporters, legal
reporters, political reporters, arts reporters, environment reporters, perhaps – but always reporters.

The reference in the last paragraph, it should be noted, was
to one 'editor', not to one 'Editor'. Until journalists abandon
the belittling trick, which is worth looking at in more detail, of
terming politicians on the printed page the prime minister, the
foreign secretary or the home secretary rather than the Prime
Minister, the Foreign Secretary or the Home Secretary, some
members of the public may think it would be more honest and
less tricksy if journalists applied fewer capital letters and fancy
titles to themselves. Rather than being the reporter's fault, the
practice may have been inspired by the top brass of the newspaper, and passed on by the sub-editors handling a reporter's
copy. But all are journalists, or should be.

If a publication refers to a nation's political chief as the
prime minister, but calls its own editorial chief the Editor, its
more cynical readers might consider that the same practice, if

it came from some public figure, would be denounced by it as hypocritical.

There is a strong case for saying that the best journalism is strong on facts and reasonable interpretation, and less strong on self-importance. More rarely than in the past do you see middle-aged reporters who have done the job all their professional lives and regard it as a badge of achievement. At the present time, many national reporters appear to be young toffs doing a task that is regarded as menial on their way to doing something better. Does this situation tempt them to lend themselves, as mere reporters without a capital letter, to self-serving sensational practices?

It is also worth examining further the tricks that can be played with capital letters and the lack of them: what in print journalism is known as upper-case letters and lower-case letters.

4

Upper and Lower Case

When you see, in a newspaper or magazine, journalists giving upper-case letters to themselves and lower-case letters to other people, you may be excused for asking what trick is being played.

No doubt some critics of the media would describe it as simple megalomania, of the same sort as some media tycoons displayed in the 1980s, when their new maxim was: 'We will decide the news agenda of the day.' No doubt I was not the only one who wanted to ask them, 'How many air crashes a month would you prescribe?' or 'How many changes of government would you arrange in a year?' Nor do I think that I was the only person who felt that that proposition went way beyond the usual and wise limits of journalism, which in its healthiest form consists of following the news stories of the day as they break, and commenting on them separately, if required.

Those friendly to journalists may argue that reducing the

working titles of politicians and other public figures to lower-case letters instead of using initial capitals is part of a democratization process in an age which prides itself on being democratic so long as its own privileges are not being interfered with. The suggestion would be that if you call the Prime Minister the prime minister, he becomes less 'elitist' and more 'approachable', 'accessible', or any other of those fey and patronizing 'buzzwords' through which we are led to believe that, if we reduce the status of others in an attempt to magnify our own, the world will somehow be a more friendly and manageable place – rather than simply a more confused and anarchic one.

If the editor of the newspaper expressing such a view is referred to as the Editor, such a self-interested argument is immediately exposed as self-deluding. The trick here is simply reductionism: journalists talking themselves up by talking everyone else down, a trick with many variations that all add up to the same thing.

The trouble is that when it is the rich and powerful who are thus reduced to lower-case letters, it is easy to see why the process is so popular and, in one sense, defensible. When I first entered journalism, politicians did not have the 'spin' mechanisms they employ today. They often spoke in public halls. They could be heckled, and they often were. They could be, and were, approached by reporters after their speeches to clear up any points that were thought to be unclear, or to elaborate on any points of particular interest. They did not operate in the hermetically sealed conditions of the television studio. They were not, unless they were Russian or American politicians on foreign soil, surrounded by posses of minders, communications directors (definitely with *their* capital letters), hairdressers and style-advisers.

Newspapers and television may have some reason for arguing that they have been pushed as far as tolerably possible towards the periphery of political events, unless their presence should be thought to be conducive to the politicians' own interests. But if the reduction of the Prime Minister and the Home Secretary to the prime minister and the home secretary is part of a response to that, it is surely a feeble, petulant and petty response that, especially in the case of newspapers and magazines, does their readers no favours.

Readers appreciate clarity. Perhaps if the journalist writes about the prime minister, it is still clear that the head of government is being referred to. But if you are faced with a home secretary, you may imagine a secretary who is employed in the home rather than in the office. If your eye encounters a foreign secretary, you may at first be tempted to wonder whether he is French, German or Spanish. If your eye encounters the archbishop of Canterbury, you may well wonder how long it will be before he becomes the archbishop of canterbury. If the proper name of a human functionary does not warrant an initial capital letter, why should the name of a town or city be so favoured? Or your name, my name, or the name of any private individual?

Reductionism is a fashion that can be irritating while achieving nothing, except to indicate that a game of supremacy is being played. At its most irritating, it can be a trick against the eye and the senses. It may deprive the reader of helpful signposts that will make his progress quicker and surer as he reads.

Which of these two paragraphs is the easier to absorb?

1. The prime minister said yesterday that he would order an enquiry into allegations by the national audit office that the foreign secretary had misled the home secretary over the costs to the national health service of the current flow of refugees.

Or

2. The Prime Minister said yesterday that he would order an enquiry into allegations by the National Audit Office that the Foreign Secretary had misled the Home Secretary over the costs to the National Health Service of the current flow of refugees.

Surely the reader is much better able to find his way around the second version than the first? The first is a blank expanse of grey type with no signposts, no immediately recognizable reference points that make the subject matter crystal clear. The reader is not immediately able to judge the importance of the story.

The second version gives due importance to the public figures and public bodies concerned. This is not merely to flatter the perhaps pompous people concerned: it is inspired primarily by consideration for the reader rather than for the public persons and institutions described. It is more arresting than the same thing rendered with lower case initials, and helps the reader to visualize the people concerned in clear images.

But let us be frank. Using upper-case letters at the beginning of descriptions of offices held can definitely make them seem more important. And usually they *should* seem more important. The position of Prime Minister is important and it should always be treated as if it were. If its importance is contested or belittled, on what other basis can the Prime Minister be persistently questioned and held to public account?

The game of lower-case reductionism played in many quarters of the print media may be not only petty but, above all, illogical. The claim that it is 'healthy' for public figures to be reduced in this way is directly contrary to the truth. The moral truth is that their importance must always be acknowledged before they can be effectively criticized. The technical truth is that prime ministers, home secretaries and archbishops of canterburys make the reader's task more difficult and less pleasurable.

It may be argued today, when many people in newspaper offices are styled as 'editors' of one sort or another, the only way to describe the chief editorial executive is as the Editor. It is a seductive argument, and a convincing one if the publication concerned confers equal dignity on other people. Otherwise, it can be specious.

Lower-case reductionism can be an attempt by media people to belittle public figures; to bring them down nearer to the stature of people in journalism and the street. The existence of the Editor, when the Prime Minister is routinely deprived of his own capital letters, is a reliable give-away.

Two generations ago, people became journalists, on the whole, because they were no good at anything else, or because economic or other factors had stunted their education. They could not have become qualified doctors, barristers, solicitors, architects. This militated against them becoming self-important. Today, as we have seen, journalism has become a glamorous occupation, often attracting personable hot-shots and misfit toffs who should ideally be doing more justice to their talents or at least to their vanity – by joining the Cabinet, captaining productive industries, leading men in battle, administering the Colonies, and that sort of thing.

It has never been more vital for us to have journalists who engage in dedicated and effective questioning of our masters rather than in posturing tricks like awarding themselves, but no one else, the distinction of upper-case letters.

However, other tricks involving the deployment of words can be even more questionable.

5

Prejudicial Words

Few news stories, even in the local press about the local bee-keeping club, let alone in national journalism, are now considered complete without an intro (a first paragraph) suggesting some form of failure, hypocrisy, double-dealing or other scandal which the publication concerned is ruthlessly exposing in the service of its readers. 'No infamy, no horror, no skulduggery, no story' has become a widespread maxim and, since infamy and horror are not the sole ingredients of life, they tend to be supported by tricks with words to imply the worst.

The habit of 'telling it as it is' has been compromised by some news desks appearing to think that there is no news story at all unless there is something nasty involved. That, at any rate, is what many members of the public who have to deal with journalists on a more than casual basis now believe, even if they do not confide their suspicions to working journalists. Why should they prejudice their own working relationships with them? Far too risky! Any journalist who doubts the presence of such suspicions in the public mind should at least try to get an honest view on this issue from his contacts.

Here are two ways of introducing a news story:

1. The government yesterday announced its plans for reducing class sizes in junior schools to no more than twenty. They are: etc, etc, etc.

Or

2. The government's plans, announced yesterday, for reducing class sizes in junior schools to no more than twenty are deeply flawed and bound to fail. Such is the opinion of some teachers who told the *Daily Investigator* yesterday that they would not cooperate and charged the government with rank hypocrisy ...

The first approach enables the reader to learn what the government's proposals *are* before the assorted and asserted reasons why they will not work are set out. The second is more contemporarily typical in that it finds fault with the subject of the story before that subject has even been described fully for the reader.

Notice the sleight of hand involved in the second example, including the casual use of the word 'charged'. There are a number of derogatory buzz-words which imply a scandal even when the later recounted facts do not fully substantiate them: 'charged' is one of the most over-employed. The only correct use of the word 'charged' is in connection with a criminal offence. If you have been caught with your hand in the till, you may well be charged. If you have knocked someone down while driving with more than the legal amount of alcohol in your blood, you may be charged. If you sign someone else's name on a cheque for your own benefit, you may be charged.

All these reasons for being charged imply something criminal. Thus, by association, the use of the word 'charged' implies that something discreditable is involved. The word's use in many news stories is fraudulent when there has been no legal charge at all, and nothing remotely like a reason for one. The most the second intro could legitimately aspire to would be:

Such is the opinion of some teachers who told the *Daily Investi-*

gator yesterday that they would not cooperate, and alleged that the government was guilty of hypocrisy.

Even the use of the word 'allege' can be prejudicial, dignifying a partisan position with a quasi-judicial status. But it is less prejudicial than 'charged' and may be the best word even a conscientious journalist can use in a particular set of circumstances.

Having focused on 'charged' and seen through its pretensions, the clear-sighted may well find that other derogatory buzz-words become more easily detectable.

'Plea' is a case in point. When someone asks for something (to which he may well be legitimately entitled), he may be discredited by a reference to his 'plea' for this, that or the other. At the worst, it will imply that he is in some form of judicial proceedings, in which he is entering a plea of not guilty although he may be guilty. At the very least, it will imply that he has lost his dignity to the extent that he is whining. 'Plea' is a word which can make its utterer sound pathetic.

'Defeat' is another deceptive word. It is part of a media process by which every issue, large or small, is turned into a pitched battle between individuals or groups, a conversion which has (from some sections of the media's point of view) the desirable result of making a story more profitably 'accessible' to the duller-witted.

Consider this example:

> The government suffered a defeat yesterday at the hands of its own back-benchers when it bowed to their pressure and announced that it would revise its plans, on which not all members of the government are agreed, for privatizing the police. The expected plans, modified in the light of back-bench and other pressure, will not now be debated for three months.

Did the government truly suffer a 'defeat' here? Or did it, instead, float some ideas to get a reaction and then decide to modify its plans in the light of that reaction – possibly a sensible course rather than a defeat? If modifying one's plans when it becomes obvious they are unpopular becomes a 'defeat', family rows would be even more long-lasting and destructive than they are now.

Indiscriminate and inaccurate use of the word 'defeat' in journalism is a trick that makes the conduct of civilized life more difficult than it need be. Everyone becomes determined that they should not be seen to do anything that might conceivably be represented as an admission of defeat. If the use of the word 'defeat' in such contexts were strictly rationed, civilized and mature decisions would be easier to reach.

Immediately the word 'defeat' is used, it is wise to ask whether it is justified. If every reader, listener and viewer did that, the baleful results of the inflammatory word would be tamed and civilized differences of opinion could be more easily contained and explained.

Similarly, the word 'outburst' is often used to spice up a story that is, in fact, not nearly so operatically dramatic. The word's use suggests that people in public life are no better than a pub crowd shouting abuse at each other at closing time, a more accurate definition of an 'outburst'. Using the same word about people in public life is no doubt flattering to the uncontrolled and unintelligent because it suggests that the eminent are really just as uncontrolled and unintelligent as they are, but it is often – or even usually – misleading.

Few men or women in any form of public life truly indulge in spontaneous and unrehearsed 'outbursts'. They would be giving too many hostages to fortune, and especially to the enemy, if they did. They measure their words, even if in the end they may use them to dramatic effect. In cases where the word 'outburst' is used in the first paragraph of a story or feature, it is not unusual to find later in the story a clear indication that nothing that could be truly described as an outburst has taken place:

> In an extraordinary outburst yesterday, the Mayor of Westbridge said he thought some people might regard the community charges in the town as on the high side.

How is this statement an 'outburst'? There is no proper basis for the use of the word here. It is a bad fashion that dictates that every slightly controversial opinion is no better than an explosion of illiterate anger from a football hooligan.

Sporting words and phrases in general should be watched carefully when they are applied to non-sporting activities. The object in almost all sports is to *win*. The winners-and-losers way of regarding life can be baleful and destructive when applied to matters other than sporting activities, even if it flatters the simple-minded into thinking they understand public issues. Because it implies that decisions are about fighting for supremacy rather than for an intellectual position, it can make definitive thought and judgment difficult or impossible.

Faced with any sporting word or phrase in a non-sporting context, the reader, listener or viewer should ask himself: is there a trick being played here, and if so what is it? Is it constructing a barrier to understanding all the points of view involved on some issue?

'Rant', like 'outburst', is a word that is also applied freely, sometimes in circumstances that do not justify it. It is a feature writer's rather than a reporter's term, and is often used with a tongue in the cheek. All the same, its use can be dangerously misleading. It can be derogatory, even if there is a pretence of light-heartedness, as in this fictitious 'rant':

> In a three-quarters of an hour rant to the British Film Institute yesterday, the Brazilian film maker Brian Vessario, who is having difficulty financing his latest film, accused Hollywood of being obsessed with money and abnormal psychology instead of cinematic art; the British film industry of being a feeble, lack-lustre and aridly academic satellite of Hollywood; and the French film industry of being self-conscious and parochial.

In what way, one should immediately ask, were those opinions a 'rant'? On the contrary, whether they were right or wrong, each of the three opinions would be easily defensible in the eyes of many people who go to the cinema. Even putting all three together in the course of a three-quarters of an hour lecture does not make the result a 'rant'. Even the fact that the fictitious Brazilian film-maker has a vested interest in getting his own film financed does not make what he says a 'rant'. And the attack on the British film industry when he is talking to a British audience certainly does not make it a 'rant'.

The use of the word, even when it is used in a tongue-in-the-cheek sense, is merely an attempt to imply that an intellectual position frankly stated is no more than belligerent hot air. It is part of a campaign, conscious or unconscious, to reduce the elements of an intellectual argument to a melodramatic and personalized explosion.

'Gaffe' (a blundering mistake) is another trick word that requires careful watching, as it is often used about behaviour which is not necessarily a mistake at all, let alone a blundering one. It is a word that can be applied to any behaviour which commands attention, irrespective of the fact that many people might regard the behaviour as perfectly sensible. If a criminal were using the word, he might well apply it to an act of self-sacrifice or honesty. The children who pointed out to the pompous Emperor that he was not wearing the fine clothes he thought to be invisible to all those without good taste, but was in fact naked, might have been accused of a gaffe. They were not guilty of one. They just happened to be the first to point out something that other people were too frightened to mention.

In 2006, the newly appointed Home Secretary, the habitually outspoken John Reid, was said by some newspapers to have committed a gaffe by saying that a judge's sentence imposed for a serious crime against a child was too lenient. The judge had recommended a five-year 'tariff' (or possibly reduced sentence) for a man who had been found guilty of abducting and seriously assaulting sexually a three-year-old girl, whose parents were upset and angered by what they regarded as far too lenient a punishment. The paedophile committed the offence when he was out of prison on a 'supervised licence' after being found guilty of assaulting a six-year-old in 2003.

It may well have been the custom that the Home Secretary should be debarred by his office from uttering such a sentiment. But did that mean that overriding that inhibition was automatically a 'gaffe'? The possibility that the Home Secretary might well have known the legal niceties but had chosen to ignore them in this particular case in the greater interest of common sense was perhaps too subtle a possibility to carry a headline. The Attorney General, Lord Goldsmith, had at about this time drawn up a list of two hundred judges who were criticized for lenient sentencing. Was caring more for justice than the strict protocol of his office as Home Secretary a crass blunder on the part of John Reid: a 'gaffe'? Is it a point to be debated rather than decided by the choice of an arbitrary word in a newspaper report?

Jesus's Sermon on the Mount and Abraham Lincoln's Gettysberg Address could easily be represented as 'gaffes', especially if the first were being assessed by ambitious hedge-fund managers and the second by those who would have preferred a perpetually divided America. 'Gaffe' is a prejudicial word that has become deeply suspect.

Some journalists seek to defend their 'dreadful or nothing' choice of words to describe what is happening in the world by pointing out – quite correctly – that it is the job of the press and other media to report on the one plane that crashes, not the thousands that don't; the one company director who indulges in fraud, not the thousands who don't; the one politician who is caught uttering a downright lie, not the hundreds who don't; the one minister who resigns from the government, not the dozens who don't.

All of that is perfectly true. But it is not the same thing as saying that only disaster can make a news story, and definitely not the same thing as trying to imply, by the choice of prejudicial rather than exact words, that people or situations are worse than they are.

Such trick prejudicial words, in so far as they achieve anything, tend to make public hysteria respectable. The wise reader, listener or viewer will regard them with extreme caution and, if they are not supported by specific facts in any particular case, will disregard them.

Even if another example of word manipulation in the next chapter can be an overdone irritant rather than a social menace, it may discourage the public from taking the perpetrators as seriously as they should be and could be taken.

6

Puns

'Transport chief derailed'. Or perhaps 'Aircraft shares nose-dive'. Or 'Dentist fills top post'. All readers of journalism must have come across this trick half a dozen times and been charmed by it; and then, several hundred times later, had their teeth set on edge by it.

It is tempting to regard the constant use of puns or play on words in print-media headings as an underhand trick, perpetrated by disaffected workers within the print media, to persuade their readers to leave newspapers and magazines on the news-stand and rely solely on radio, the internet or television – although otherwise interesting collectors' programmes (as distinct from journalism) like BBC TV's *Bargain Hunt* and *Cash in the Attic* can be persistent tongue-in-the-cheek offenders.

If this theory will not hold water, it is difficult to see why the use of puns and play on words is now so popular a trick in newspapers and magazines. When it was first tried in the Swinging Sixties, the practice had an air of original, humorous and witty irreverence. In the third millennium, it has sometimes taken on the appearance of a frantic jesting trick performed by a street busker in the vain hope of claiming attention from a disappearing audience.

Let us imagine that a newspaper wants to indicate opposition to a government's plans partly to increase the privatization element in the London Underground, believing that the government has not foreseen the dangers to proper maintenance and safety. This is a serious issue which it might be thought that any intelligent reader would be prepared to read about without artificial incentives. But with gritted teeth, imagine the possible punning headings that could be put on such a story. You will almost certainly be right in assuming that some newspaper will put up the heading: 'Government on wrong train'. Another will come up with: 'Government are sleepers'. And yet another will announce: 'Government on wrong track'. Or simply: 'Government down the tube'.

By the time the average reader has read the day's coverage of this issue and others that have been similarly treated, he will very probably feel like protesting: 'For heaven's sake, just tell me in straightforward terms what has happened, and stop trying to make a clumsy clever-clever simpering joke of everything.'

Is play on words now a trick that has been over-used by professionals because they are themselves sick and tired of the day's news and want any sort of laugh as light relief? This might be excusable in a layman but it is not in a journalist. It would be even more inexcusable if the journalist assumed that the reader shared his languid cynicism. In practice, the reader may well be tired, not of the news, but of attempts to introduce a snigger where no sniggering rationally belongs, where the chirpy use of words that can have more than one meaning can be an irritation.

As an indication of how extensively the trick has spread, here are some examples from *one* issue of a quality broadsheet daily newspaper, *The Times* of 16 March 2005, a date chosen at random:

Page 2. 'A snip at £3,120'. This was the heading on a story about a lock of Charles Dickens's hair raising £3,120 at a London auction.

Page 7. 'Taxpayers' Arctic art cuts no ice with critic'. A heading over a story about the British taxpayer paying for the artist Anthony Gormley to build a snowman in the Arctic, even though only a few polar bears would see it. David Lee, the editor of *The Jackdaw*, the satirical art magazine, commented, 'It's a long way away and nobody can see it.'

Page 10. 'Cell discovery could put cancer to sleep'. The story here was about scientists who had devised a way of putting cancer cells into a state resembling sleep, so that they did not proliferate.

Page 13. 'Putin in check'. A gossip paragraph about the Russian chess-master Garry Kasparov vowing to stop Vladimir Putin having a third term in office.

And so on. There were further punning headings on pages 25, 27, 31, 41, 42, 59, 67 and 69, though this did not include the *appropriately* jokey heading to Alan Coren's humorous column, entitled 'Which came first, the chicken or this feeling that my days are numbered?'

We have established that punning headings to stories are not the sole prerogative of the red-top tabloid national newspapers. Are regional and local newspapers, which used to be more down-to-earth, even sombre, than their national counterparts, free of the trick? They are not. It would be more true to say that what the national newspapers did yesterday the regional and local newspapers will do today.

As an example, we will examine one issue, 18 March 2005, of the broadsheet *Brentford Chiswick & Isleworth Times*, which can lay claim to being a quality newspaper that takes its responsibilities to the community seriously.

'Tennis courts saga in extended play'. This was the heading above a page 1 story about dilapidated tennis courts at Chiswick Back Common that were due for redevelopment, but where workmen had not arrived. This left the courts 'characterized by empty beer-cans, used condoms and a distinct lack of tennis players'. Perhaps the residents in the immediate area were less amused by the 'extended play' pun than other readers.

'Plant the seeds of the future'. A page 3 story about how residents on a Hounslow estate were being invited to plant a tree to help start an urban forest to improve their local area.

'Stamping their mark on charity's good work'. A story on page 4 about how a 'first class' performance by fund-raisers at a local delivery firm, TNT Express Services, had resulted in the company delivering its biggest-ever donation to a charity appeal for used stamps.

' "Mr Benn" finds an outfit to suit him'. A page 8 story about how a lifeboat helmsman had found an 'outfit' to suit him – i.e. an organization as well as a mode of safety attire that 'suited' him – two puns for the price of one.

And there were three more punning headings in that single issue. Some readers will no doubt find the punning entertaining and an encouragement to read on. It is not a dangerous trick, nor even necessarily a tasteless one; but it can become tiresome and irritating with excessive use, especially if there is a suggestion of it being contrived. There is also some risk that

material which features it may not be taken with the serious-
ness it should be taken: some things in real life are simply not
a laughing matter and ideally should not be laced with tortuous word-play to make them more 'accessible', however much
the people who wrote the headings may be hugging themselves
with joy at their own cleverness.

Or, as others might or might not say, should contrivers of
punning headings be beheaded? Ha, ha, ha, ha. Not.

Though puns in headings may have a value in inverse proportion to their frequency, the results of this sort of word
manipulation will be, at worst, a mere irritation to the reader.
The manipulation of questions asked and of answers given in
the course of reporting is a trick with more serious implications.

7

Concealing the Questions

Reporter: 'Archbishop, on your first visit to New York, are you
going to investigate the brothels?'
Archbishop of Canterbury (politely): 'Are there any brothels in
New York?'
Beginning of subsequent newspaper report: 'On his first visit to
New York, the Archbishop of Canterbury's first question was:
"Are there any brothels in New York?"'

That, of course, was pure fiction. But it has a very real point.
As a reader, before you can evaluate an *answer*, you ideally
need to know the precise *question* that was asked. Eliminating
all signs of the question, even eliminating all signs that a question was asked at all and making it look as if a statement was
volunteered out of the blue, is a journalistic trick that can have
unfair consequences. Some reportage is misleading, at least in
tone if not in literal fact, because it uses a remark someone has
made without explaining its context, the most important part

of which may well relate to the nature of a journalist's question, or questions that led up to it.

It used to be possible in some quality newspapers for a reporter to write stories in which both questions and answers were clearly and fully quoted. A reporter could write like this:

> When asked, 'Are there any circumstances at all in which you would consider resigning?' the minister said: 'There are no circumstances at present which would lead me to consider resignation.'

Such a reply, purged of the question that provoked it, can be used to create a misleading impression in more than one way. Here are a few possibilities:

> Attacked from all sides for his inaccurate report to the House of Commons on the refugee situation last week, the Home Secretary brazenly pointed the two fingers of scorn at his critics by saying that there were 'no circumstances' in which he would consider resignation.

This version makes him out to be not a man politely answering a question but an unheeding oaf who despises public opinion.

Or:

> Hopes that the Home Secretary might resign in the face of recent criticisms of his inaccurate statement on refugees to the House of Commons last week grew yesterday when he said that there were no circumstances 'at present' in which he would consider resignation – thus opening up the possibility that he might do so later.

In both these less than totally honest versions, there is no indication that the minister was not volunteering a statement off his own bat, but only answering a specific question posed by a journalist.

Making the question's wording so provocative that the contact responds with an emphatic answer including the words that made the question provocative, which answer is then reported without any mention of the question that inspired the emphatic answer, is a journalist's trick that may in some quarters be considered permissible. Surely those who presume to go into public life at national or local level should not fall for traps like that?

Perhaps not. It is a sad fact that today's politicians are so drilled in media-handling that few things pop out of their lips by accident, even the truth. Perhaps in some circumstances it is legitimate for a journalist to pose a provocative or trick question in pursuit of the truth. What is not legitimate is that there should then be a contrived pretence that the question was never asked, and that the remarks quoted were made spontaneously. Would the journalist like it if someone asked him, 'Are you facing the sack?', he replied, 'I am not facing the sack,' and then someone reported that he had just denied that he was facing the sack, thus implying that it was a possibility?

In what were once called 'human interest' stories, in the days before 'human interest' came too often to mean little more than 'sex or sleaze interest', the angry remark by one party to a divorce could be especially suspect because it was almost bound to be the result of a reporter's provocative question.

> Journalist: 'What are you going to do now you have got rid of your philandering shit of a husband?'
> Divorcee: 'My philandering shit of a husband can go to hell as far as I am concerned.'
> Report: 'My philandering shit of a husband can go to hell as far as I am concerned,' said …

No doubt many contemporary journalists would argue that reporting the questions as well as the answers would be 'archaic' and 'rambling'. It is certainly true that the technique requires more space, and that the pressure on editorial space is especially severe now that more and more lucrative advertisements – instead of more and more truthful journalism – are the principal ambition of some proprietors.

But there are circumstances where not quoting a question

before reporting the answer can be a particularly misleading form of trickery, and it is one the reader, listener or viewer should always bear in mind.

The reader is well advised to ask himself a few questions. Are the words quoted ones which that person would be likely to volunteer? If not, could it be that the words were put into his mouth by a question that has not been quoted? If the statement uses a word or words that are sensational, and not easily to be associated with the person being questioned, is it possible that they were contained in the undeclared question and were merely repeated carelessly by the person questioned, or not specifically rebutted by him?

'I am not guilty of lying' may easily appear to be the remark of a liar defending himself if the reader is unaware that the specific question, 'Are you guilty of lying?' has been asked. In looking at all apparent statements, it is wise to ask what question or questions could have precipitated them, and to judge the result with some caution.

Even more dangerous is the trick of attributing words to a person when all he has done is to say 'Yes,' to a form of words put to him by a journalist. The journalist may say, 'Minister, is it true that you have worked your cotton socks off to settle this issue?' And the minister may well be in a hurry and reply simply, 'Yes.' But suppose the resultant report read:

'I have worked my cotton socks off to settle this issue,' the minister said yesterday.

Would the report be fair, especially if the minister was not the sort of man to use such semi-literate slang? Being credited with uttering such a sentiment could make him seem plaintive and perhaps not up to his job, as well as semi-literate. It is possible that such 'statements' are not quite what they seem.

Other, totally different, statements that are made in the course of journalistic contact may conceal an even more suspect trick, though fortunately it is rarer.

8

Puffery

The most obvious danger of self-interested puffing, in what masquerades as an objective report, lies in reporting on shares and other investments. It is only one way in which an unscrupulous journalist can puff from a privileged position; but it is one of the few from which a direct financial profit can be made. To be fair, most journalistic tricks are not concerned with money but with producing desired effects on the page or screen.

The trick for any opportunist in journalism hoping to make money for himself by speculation lies in puffing shares that he holds and then selling them at the increased value that is produced by his puffing. If he is careful as well as opportunistic, he will do this only in ways that can be objectively defended. So that even if his own share dealing is discovered, he can explain away what he wrote by saying that it was objectively true. If a journalist says that a particular share is a good buy at a time when other financial journalists are saying the same thing, no one is likely to assume that he is puffing the shares only because he owns some, or knows someone who owns some, and wants to see them increase in value.

Similarly, if he puffs the shares of a large company that is important to Britain's prosperity, he can always claim that he is motivated by patriotism rather than by the fact that he owns some of the shares himself, or knows someone who does. In such cases, it might be difficult to establish his predominant motive with any certainty.

The difference between giving an objective judgment on a particular share and puffing investments in which a journalist has invested can be a very fine one indeed. That is why scams in this area are so difficult to deal with but, one would assume, small in number.

Let us say that journalist X, after reporting on the upward progress of British Brilliant Ball Bearings after a slump in its fortunes, has acquired two thousand such shares for 105p each

– hardly more than they were quoted for on the Stock Exchange at the nadir of the company's misfortunes. He continues to report in highly favourable terms on the company's progress in cutting costs, eliminating debt and finding new markets. Perhaps he specifically urges readers, listeners or viewers to buy the shares. Within two months the shares have risen to 205p, and he sells his own, producing a profit of 100p a share or £2,000 for his holding.

Irrespective of the journalist's newspaper's specific rules, is this corruption or not? It is difficult to be dogmatic. The journalist may well claim that he would have written about the company and its shares exactly as he did even if he had not personally owned shares in it. And he might well have done just that. The journalist's original belief in the company may have been quite genuine: other media people may have praised British Brilliant Ball Bearings; the company could be considered to be an important one to Britain and its interests.

It is only when he comes to sell the shares to take a profit that the big question hovers: even if journalists are entitled to make investments, should they be long-term rather than short-term ones, in order to dispel any suggestion of 'playing the markets' from a privileged position? If the director of a company with 'inside information' were to buy or sell shares in accordance with that knowledge, he would find himself in trouble. Journalists, especially specialized ones, are sometimes very close to 'inside information'.

But suppose journalist X avoids selling his shares to raise a quick profit and instead holds on to them. He is not thus automatically removed from all temptation. Suppose also that some months later the company share price sags again, finishing up at 55p – representing a paper loss to the journalist of 50p a share, or £1,000 on his investment.

Then suppose that in these circumstances journalist X continues to praise and talk up British Brilliant Ball Bearings and its share price at a time when other pundits are writing them down or off? Journalist X may still be able to argue that this was his genuine belief and no one could say, without getting inside his head, that this was not true. But there might be a suspicion of corruption or trickery in the mind of anyone who knew that he had invested in the company, and journalist X would not be able to *prove* the contrary.

If journalists are able to buy shares about which they are writing, it may in many instances be impossible either to prove or disprove corrupt or highly self-interested rather than purely journalistic motives. Media organizations may have their own rules, but the only way to make it clear to the public that their journalists are not playing tricks would be to establish a watertight rule that journalists writing about shares, or journalists able to influence from a superior organizational position those writing about shares, should not themselves invest in them or sell existing holdings, except perhaps through a 'blind trust' such as politicians set up for their own investments when they assume ministerial office.

In this way, journalists could be seen not to use their own professional research and information to buy or sell their personal investments. Given the lack of such a rule applying to everyone, tricks may be suspected.

The danger of self-interested puffing, however, exists in other spheres than equities or other financial entities. At what might be thought to be the opposite philosophical extreme, those engaged in arts coverage are not automatically free either from the suspicion of tricks that imply corruption or at least self-interest – except that usually, in such a case, the corruption is intellectual rather than financial.

Suppose a journalist writes a novel, or at least something between hard covers that his publishers call a novel. Part of his work is writing about cultural matters: he has very wide freedom in his choice of subject. Does the identity of the publisher of his novel affect the way he writes about that publisher and its books or, indeed, its main rivals? Does he puff the works of his publisher and damn the works of its main rivals?

There is an important difference here from reporting on shares in which the writer is an investor. In the case of the shares, the ownership is hidden; whereas the book, and the comments on the publisher and other publishers made by the novelist in his journalistic capacity, will be all too public. There is thus an automatic check on the novelist which there is not in the case of the investor in shares. If nine out of ten authors reported on favourably were from the journalist's own publisher, that would be unlikely to escape the attention of rival colleagues. If the author went on to sell the film rights for a substantial sum, would that diminish his independence of thought? In practice, the same checks are in place: the film and his involvement in it will not escape publicity, and if the writer suddenly finds that a director he has previously damned is now a genius, it will be a very public change of mind and one on which rivals could well comment.

For these reasons, intellectual corruption in the cultural world, including mutual back-scratching or back-stabbing, is easier to identify (and perhaps therefore less likely to occur) than financial misbehaviour in the financial world. The satirical magazine *Private Eye* is always vigilant in this respect.

It would be a mistake to assume that a self-serving trick is *necessarily* being played by a journalist just because he has some other connection with the people he is writing about. There should be no automatic assumption that a journalist will behave unfairly to publishers or producers who have spurned his novel, and that self-interestedly and dishonestly he will behave favourably towards publishers and producers who have bought his own work.

For a start, precise motives would be difficult to locate. Yes, publisher X has bought the journalist's novel, but has he given him a very small advance or not advertised the book enough, thus alienating the author rather than enthusing him? Does the journalist disapprove of the casting of the film of his book, so that he has reason to write unfavourably rather than favourably about the producer? It may be practically impossible for the reader, listener or viewer to detect with certainty any non-professional influences at work, especially any unjustified puffing of cultural activities.

That does not mean that there are not circumstances where a journalist who habitually deals with arts reporting should not stand down from reporting certain things – especially those concerning his own books, his stories or his poems. Otherwise he may in the end find himself in the position of virtually having to criticize and interview himself. Let no one bet that this will not actually happen. First-person articles about his own projects may be permissible, but they can amount to a self-promoting trick that is not easily available to a non-media person. They should accordingly be taken with a bigger pinch of salt than articles about people and activities in which the journalist himself has no personal interest.

It is not unfair to ask this question of any piece of journalism: could there be a less legitimate motive or motives behind this? If the motive is self-declared and holds water, perhaps the journalist, even if he is one you happen to find unsympathetic, will not deserve cynicism about what he writes. Few journalists are entirely strangers to sincerely held beliefs, although some may be very well acquainted indeed with the beliefs of their proprietors. It is legitimate for the public to ask of a piece of journalism: does this serve the self-interest of the journalist in any way, and even if it does not, does it serve the self-interest of the proprietor?

Sometimes what is written or broadcast in a story, even perhaps the entire story, may be generated by commercial vanity or a suspect desire for supremacy that infiltrates many aspects of journalism and explains many proud claims.

9

Firsts

On the BBC Radio 4 *Today* programme of 7 February 2004, the Acting Director-General of the BBC, Mark Byford, said that he had some sympathy with members of the public who were irritated by the BBC repeatedly claiming that parts of a programme were 'exclusive'. He thought it better to leave it to the public to decide whether a story or parts of it were 'exclusive' or not.

Perhaps the fact that he was only an 'acting' Director-General at the time enabled him to say something that someone who was an established Director-General (in effect the editor-in-chief of the BBC), or any other head of an organization, might have found it more difficult to say, for fear of alienating his staff. One way or another, it will be seen by many people as a wise comment on the self-praise and self-hyping, now commonly worked into journalism, which may or may not warrant it and which, even if it does warrant it, may have its credibility compromised by what some members of the public will regard as a sort of wine-bar boasting.

If any news organization had a story that a distinguished brain-surgeon was going to resign to become a tightrope walker in Billy Smart's Circus, they would not have to bill it as 'exclusive'. The public would know they had not heard it or seen it before, and would regard it as 'exclusive'.

In general, if a journalist really does have an exclusive story it will not be necessary for him to make the claim, or for someone else in the organization to make the claim for him. The public will know they haven't heard or seen the story before, or heard any of their friends talking about it, so that it will register with them as an 'exclusive'.

Yet we often see and hear a story, or parts of a story, being claimed as an 'exclusive' or as a 'first':

> In his first full-scale interview since his resignation, the Bishop of Bridgeford told the *Daily Investigator* yesterday that the strains within the Anglican Church had grown so considerably that his job was now too much for any one individual. He told the *Daily Investigator*: 'I have been feeling as if my brains are on fire.'

Here we have the two forms of self-congratulation we may now encounter in some form or another practically every day: that the material is exclusive to the news source, and that the interviewee has chosen this particular news organization rather than any other to speak to. In any one story, the *Daily Investigator* may be mentioned almost as often as the Bishop.

Whether the public in general is impressed by, or even notices, such self-hyping plugs would require social research to determine. Within journalism such plugs may be taken seriously as professional Brownie-points, or they may not. It is tempting to think that, as fellow-professionals, journalists would be the first to see through the pretence – and, often, the limitations – of such self-congratulation.

In the fictional 'exclusive' intro just mentioned, the claim is an illustration of how limited the claim to exclusivity or any other 'first' can be. It is boasted that the interview is the 'first full-scale' interview the Bishop of Bridgeford has given since his resignation. What is a 'full-scale' interview? Does it mean an interview in which the journalist sits down in a room alone with the person he is writing about and tape-records the interview?

Not necessarily. It could mean that the interview was in the street while the Bishop walked from his front door to his car. If both journalist and Bishop were fast talkers and the Bishop were in an obliging mood, that might have produced some valuable material – indeed some startling material. If so, the material would speak better for itself without any attempt to suggest that, whereas other competing journalists have had to make do with press handouts, the *Daily Investigator* journalist has had not only a 'full-scale' interview, whatever that means, but the 'first' full-scale interview.

By including limiting words in the 'we're first' claim, practically any such claim can avoid the Trade Descriptions legislation – at the price of making that claim hardly worth the making, especially to the reader, listener or viewer who takes stock of the precise meaning of words. Would the even more frank, 'For the first time since he gave a press conference yesterday morning, the Bishop exclusively told the *Daily Investigator* yesterday afternoon that he had no more to say except that he had enjoyed his day' convey at least a sense of humour?

Whenever something is described as an 'exclusive' or a 'first', it is wise to wonder exactly what in the content *is* exclusive or a first. If this element is so small as to be almost invisible, you are likely to have come across journalistic posturing rather than journalistic excellence.

Similarly, it may be wise to take a pinch of salt with any suggestion that the writer of a report was the *only* journalist to whom a source talked, a sort of centre in his own universe. It is certainly a 'Me! Me! Me!' era, and that has filtered through to some extent to journalism, sometimes producing a sort of raucous shout where once there was a quieter statement of self-worth – unless you happened to be Hannen Swaffer, the flamboyant columnist and spiritualist with the large battered black hat who *was* unique or somewhere near it in Fleet Street between the 1920s and the 1950s.

Swaffer could justify himself on the grounds that he was genuinely unusual. Whereas the contemporary 'Me! Me! Me!' brigade are often far too ordinary for anyone's comfort except their own. Let us explore how some of them operate.

10

He Told Me

Many journalists, as a matter of understandable professional pride and personal vanity, will try to align themselves as closely as possible with a story, suggesting at the apex of the trick that they are an integral part of it. This trick is natural in a highly competitive job, but it can be misleading.

It is true that 'My Journey Up the Congo' or 'How I Fooled the World's Leading Gun-dealers' may be rarer sorts of heading over, or even under, a personal by-line than they have been in the past, especially since sniping at largely powerless 'royals', and largely untalented and expendable 'celebrities', became a more popular and certainly a safer professional habit.

But the fact that so much contemporary journalism is not in any sense on-the-spot journalism has ironically given a new impetus to journalists who wish to assert that they are in the very thick of a story. They may be lured into taking every opportunity of writing or saying: 'He told *me* so-and-so' – though the italics here are mine in order to emphasize the point.

This could be fairly harmless – if perhaps slightly irritating after incontinent repetition – if it were the reporter himself who used the form *only* when he had personally interviewed the person he was quoting. A danger will arise if a sub-editor back at the office tries to soup up the story by introducing the 'told *me*' boast when the reporter has in fact borrowed the quote from a friendly colleague, discovered it in cuttings, got it off the internet or otherwise come by it.

What is apt to happen in such a case, especially if the quote is a contentious one, is that the person quoted will promptly and truthfully claim that he has never spoken to the reporter in question. This may be literally true, even if the quote itself is completely accurate. But the journalist cannot admit to borrowing the quote or getting it off some obscure website. Journalism is thus further discredited in the public mind – in this case, unjustly – when the quoted contact starts accusing the journalist of having *made up* the quote, on the basis that the journalist *must* have done that because the person quoted has never in his life spoken to the journalist.

Often it is the reporter himself who uses the 'told *me*' formula. One of the tricks of the trade in this context is to put the most ambitious gloss possible on even the briefest of encounters. For example, suppose that a member of the royal family announces her engagement to a naval officer, Lieutenant Nigel Upper-Lipp. The officer is serving on board the frigate HMS Livid at the time, and a press conference is arranged aboard the ship. A scrum of newspaper and electronic media people arrive on the ship at sea and surround the officer as soon as he appears. They are hustled back to a decent distance by ratings, and the press conference commences.

During it, the officer walks nervously forwards and backwards on the swaying deck and reporters and cameramen constantly shift their positions. After twenty minutes of this, the press conference is declared to be at an end, and the lieutenant is spirited away.

The next day, one report begins:

As we strolled on the swaying deck of HMS Livid yesterday, Lieutenant Nigel Upper-Lipp talked to me of his hopes and fears as he contemplates marriage to a member of the royal family.

Admire the cleverness of the sleight-of-hand. It is perfectly true that Upper-Lipp and the reporter were both on the deck of

HMS Livid. It is perfectly true that both strolled on the swaying deck – although they were a long way from one another, and separated by a crowd, at the time they did so. It is perfectly true that Nigel Upper-Lipp talked to the reporter about his hopes and fears as he contemplated marriage with a member of the royal family, even if he talked to about fifty other journalists at the same time.

Technically, the first paragraph of the story is all perfectly correct. Yet it is a trick which gives a completely false impression of what happened aboard HMS Livid. In fact, the reporter was one of a crowd of reporters and cameramen shouting on the swaying deck. From the report, we are expected to visualize the two men walking alone on the deck of HMS Livid, exchanging confidences man to man, as might two friends.

It is all too natural that reporters who go places and see things want to be *seen* as featuring prominently in the proceedings. But the 'he told *me*' formula is one to watch carefully. If the report doesn't specifically say (which it won't): 'In a one-to-one conversation yesterday as the rest of the world's media waited outside the door, So-and-So told me …', it is wisest to assume that the circumstances of the interview may not have been quite as flattering to the hard-working on-the-spot journalist as he himself wished to indicate, and that his employers gladly went along with it because it flattered the publication as well as the individual journalist.

The 'Me! Me! Me!' mode of operation in a reporter or a feature-writer may or may not indicate more ambition than talent. But, either way, it amounts to vanity rather than crookery and it is not among the most dangerously deceiving tricks that a journalist may adopt when he wants to dress up perhaps sketchy information to make it appear more well-informed and interesting.

A trick that may be more misleading, though sometimes it is played with the benevolent intention of concealing a source, is a trick of attribution or apparent attribution.

'Friends'

The use of the word 'friends' when describing unnamed informants is a useful journalistic trick. The word may or may not justify being taken literally.

Sometimes when derogatory information is laid at the door of 'friends', it makes the reader wonder what sort of 'friends' they are to indulge in such a betrayal – 'Rick has always been a selfish drunken bastard,' said a friend yesterday – and to wonder also what the sworn *enemies* of the person concerned must be like.

Sometimes the sensitive information or opinion really does come from 'friends'. But sometimes it comes from one source who is not a friend: it simply sounds more authoritative to quote a 'friend' rather than, perhaps more truthfully, an 'enemy'. Sometimes the information comes from the person himself, who for his own reasons cannot be *seen* to be speaking to journalists about the matter in hand but wants to get his views of a situation or person into the record. Sometimes it may be a more chatty way of dramatizing facts that might be thought dull if simply recounted abstractly: a quote, even from an un-named and perhaps composite or fictitious 'friend', can have more life than a baldly reported fact. These may be justifiable tricks, especially if the object is to prevent the identification of a source.

One undoubted fact remains. The reader has no possible means of knowing for sure whether the quote attributed to a 'friend' really comes from a friend or merely from someone who once saw the person who is being discussed in a pub and is exaggerating the connection to boost his own ego; or whether the quote is entirely made up from facts the reporter knows about the person featured, and he has elected to put them into the mouth of an unnamed informant to give them an air of veracity and liveliness.

In many cases, it is the subject of the remarks himself who is doing the talking. Politicians in particular have been known to give briefings to journalists on the basis that they themselves must be quoted as refusing to comment. Here it is the politician who is primarily responsible for the trickery. The journalist takes what the politician says and attributes it to an unnamed 'friend' or 'friends'.

This is the sort of thing that results:

> The Foreign Secretary will resign unless his official residence is swiftly renovated, friends said last night.
>
> They warned that the minister is so disenchanted with the repeated postponements that he regards it as a personal affront by the Prime Minister, and one that makes it difficult or impossible to do his job of entertaining foreign dignitaries.
>
> One friend said last night: 'He has had it up to here with this issue, he is absolutely disenchanted, and he now considers that the threat of resignation is the only answer left open to him.'

It would hardly come as a surprise to any journalist to hear that this story was based on a verbal briefing with the Foreign Secretary himself that went like this:

> 'This is off the record. I will resign unless my official home is swiftly renovated. I am so disenchanted with the repeated postponements that I regard it as a personal affront by the Prime Minister, and one that makes it difficult or impossible for me to do my job of entertaining foreign dignitaries. I have had it up to here with this issue and I now consider that the threat of resignation is the only answer left open to me. But all that is off the record.'

The journalist in this case has made only one give-away mistake: he has used the word 'disenchanted' to describe the Foreign Secretary's mood, ostensibly as described by 'friends'. Disenchantment is an unusual word in this context, and might well be characteristic of the Foreign Secretary himself; it is certainly sufficiently characteristic to betray the fact that it was the Foreign Secretary himself who was doing the talking.

The shrewd journalist will get round the problem of avoiding betraying the identity of the informant by 'pasteurizing' any quotes from 'friends' in such a way that distinctive give-away words are not used. This is part of the reason why so many 'friends' speak in such a slick, characterless and rather 'machined' way.

There have been publications in the past that have refused to use quotes, from 'friends' or others, unless specifically attributed. For the most part, such a high moral stance is long departed and it was perhaps always too high-minded for the real world: sometimes people say things which cast genuine light on a situation or issue, but which they are not eager to have attributed to them. But for the trick, the information or views might not reach the public. Journalists' tricks can sometimes work for the public good.

The public will have to decide for itself in every instance whether or not a trick is being played on it through the introduction of quoted 'friends', and whether the trick matters.

Is it likely that a 'friend' of the person concerned would have such a conversation with the reporter concerned? 'A friend of a distinguished politician told *Tit and Bum Magazine* yesterday it was ridiculous to suggest that he had washed his feet in the sink of a Brussels hotel ...' Is it likely?

Do the rhythms of the sentences quoted have a genuine ring, or do the words sound as if they could not have been spoken except by an electronic machine? 'A friend said yesterday: "The circumstances do not vouchsafe much promise for a bilateral solution."'

Does the quote include things that no one except the brain-damaged would utter? As in this case: 'A friend said yesterday: "My wife, forty-five-year-old Ellen, has long been a friend of the red-haired Duchess, fifty-nine, and has never noticed her drinking to excess."'

All those quotes from 'friends' are suspect simply because, if they had been lines of dialogue in a play, they would have been unconvincing and provoked a strike among the actors since the words were difficult to utter: it is simply not how people, certainly not 'friends', actually speak.

It might be unfair to deny journalists completely the 'friends' formula for conveying information and comment. But the fact is that though it may not necessarily be an unforgivably

SHOVEL IT ALL IN

dishonest trick, there is no sure means by which the public can tell whether or not it *is* a dishonest trick. All unattributed quotes and sources should perhaps be regarded with a measure of caution, especially when they are part of the trick in which unnamed 'friends' are invoked.

Regurgitated and reconstituted facts, as distinct from original research, are a lazier trick, and it is one which possibly has greater dangers.

12

Shovel It All In

Examine any ten examples of newspaper or magazine feature articles that happen to catch your eye. Read them carefully. How many of them show evidence of being based on any original research, as distinct from press-cuttings, website information and other souvenirs of the past?

The computer and the internet have made respectable what was once referred to scornfully in live journalism as a 'cuttings job'. It now seems perfectly respectable to sit in front of a screen manipulating material from one electronic source or file into another file, and having the result printed. One of the penalties of doing this is that some of the 'cuttings' and other sources may contain errors that were corrected at the time without the correction being preserved.

During the second world war, the shortage of paper led to there being newspapers of only twelve pages or fewer. Sometimes it is tempting to think that we *still* have newspapers of twelve pages or fewer – except that they now run to 120 pages. Much of the balance is 'style' journalism, which some readers regard as padding. Celebrities may tell at length how they tie their neckties or why they prefer the colour black to the colour brown; or the colour brown to the colour black. These are 'opinion pieces', which emit more heat than light, and features which rehash facts to illuminate current prejudices.

This is lazy journalism, which is sometimes perpetrated as a self-defensive trick by journalists who are forced to write too hastily, or too much – especially if they are 'celebrities' whose media paymasters want to show them off in every conceivable slot in order to get their money's worth.

At its best, journalism consists of going to a spot where something is happening and coming back with the best possible report on *what* is happening. At the opposite pole to this is the 'shovel it all in' trick, in which very few new facts, if any, are used as a lead-in to a re-hash of yesterday's, last week's or last year's news. As a way of filling the space between the advertisements of lucratively large newspapers and other publications it may be economically acceptable, but it does not encourage the highest journalistic standards.

In today's conditions, where speed is thought to be of the essence, it is understandable that going to see people has become unpopular: it takes time for even the fastest taxi or hire car to get there. How much more 'plugged-in' is it for a journalist to sit in the office in front of a screen and shovel into his report what is appearing on it from the news agencies, plus back-up material from the internet! In this way he stays in the office and is able to defend his back in all the inevitable office politics. Objectively, he may be able to claim that in the office he is at the *centre* of a news-gathering web, whereas if he goes out of the office into the world he will see only one aspect of a story. If he is a freelance, the benefits of staying in his own office are obvious: he can juggle better with two or more stories at once.

There are any number of excuses for not going out on a story, and electronics have provided some of the most powerful ones. It is true that through the internet, or from other sources, a journalist can reliably cobble together some sort of story, even if it is based on material available to everyone else. It is also true that diligently fingering a keyboard in front of a screen seems much more 'contemporary' than speaking on the telephone to an actual human being, or even talking to one face to face far away from the office.

Fortunately the 'shovel it all in' trick is easy to recognize. Are there any direct quotes in the story, and do some of them relate to what has happened yesterday or today? If there are, it indicates that the journalist may actually have talked to somebody. Reams of comment about so-and-so's 'position' or 'known views', unsupported by direct quotes, may indicate a resumé from yesterday's or last week's newspapers.

Some journalists are better than others at contriving relevance for facts which are less than new. The more skilful ones can present yesterday's news so cleverly cemented to today's that you can hardly see the join. The fact remains that facts and quotes gathered personally *today* are the best journalism, and that the rest can easily veer towards space-filling, which in itself can be a trick played on a pliant public.

The decreasing use of today's original and attributed quotes as the backbone of stories and features has led some journalists who do pursue original material to commit a different sort of irritating trick, which is to write as much, or more, about their own skill at getting the quotes as about the quotes themselves, producing those 'exclusive' or otherwise hyped facts that have been previously discussed. The search for facts, rather than the day's facts themselves, becomes the essence of the dramatic story.

However, it may be thought to be on the whole a less undesirable trick to boast about attempts to discover new facts and quotes than not to discover any. With enough new facts and quotes in his notebook, a journalist is less likely to gather past stories and quotes and perform the trick of 'shovelling it all in'.

There is one type of phrase or arrangement of words which should never be 'shovelled in', or indeed be allowed in at all – yet it is one which repeatedly occurs in print, radio and television journalism, despite its identity as a mental crutch.

13

Let Me Through, I'm a Cliché

Facts are sometimes distorted because a journalist, almost as a nervous reflex, seeks the comfort of a cliché in an intro and then strains to make the facts fit.

Clichés are at worst the refuge of people who do not even *want* to think freshly and originally. In a pub near closing time, clichés may be relatively harmless. On the printed page or when broadcast they can be annoying intellectual menaces that encourage readers, listeners or viewers to think only along stereotyped tramlines and never venture away into independent and realistic thought.

If the journalist does not consciously resist it, a cliché may barge its way to the fore like a doctor trying to get to an accident. Some newspapers apparently encourage clichés deliberately. Presumably this is because it flatters the readers by presenting them, in the celebrity circus of the media, with clichés like the clichés they hear at closing time in their wine bar. It is wise to beware. Clichés do not exist independently, with no bearing on what surrounds them: they can distort or blunt the truth of what is being described or discussed.

The adjectival and verbal cliché, so easy to coin, is a special culprit:

> Livid housewife Mrs Flora Blank (37) yesterday flayed her local council for not emptying refuse bins for three weeks in the sheltered cul-de-sac in which she lives with her irate husband Fred (38).

Here we have three clichés in one sentence – and three which are very difficult to live up to: 'livid', 'flayed' and 'irate'. Though Mrs Blank may be a reasonable woman, and have a good case, immediately the journalist uses these three dramatic clichés in his intro, he puts himself under pressure to follow it up with proof that Mrs Blank is livid and is 'flaying' her local council, and that her husband is 'irate'.

The word 'livid' suggests that everything Mrs Blank says will be said in a heated way, so that every word she utters will be represented as a tirade, when in fact she may have made her observations quietly and reasonably.

The use of another, even more popular, irritating cliché, 'devastated', may transform a perfectly sensible and adequate person into a whining wreck. This sort of thing is familiar:

> Mother of three Charlotte Nought said yesterday that she was devastated when her public library refused to order for her one of her seven-year-old daughter's favourite books.
>
> 'It is narrow-mindedness on the part of the council, and I am devastated and gutted by it,' she said.

Mrs Nought is dabbling in misleading clichés and so is the journalist reporting her. Mrs Nought wants to whip up sympathy for herself and the journalist wants a sensational story, or as near a sensational story as he can make it.

Devastated? Someone who is devastated will have suffered such a blow that all her normal composure has collapsed and she has been reduced to a gibbering and twitching wreck, or an inert lump. Is it being seriously suggested that Mrs Nought, as the result of the public library declining to stock a children's book, has been reduced to that condition?

Similarly with 'gutted'. Perhaps at the abrupt end of a passionate love affair, or on the accidental death of her child, Mrs Nought might have felt as if all her intestines had been ripped out and fallen to the ground – but it could hardly have been because of the council's policy on the books it is and is not prepared to order and stock.

Clichés can lead to stereotyping because they reduce the person being reported on to a stylized, and often melodramatic, phantom. If clichés are used early enough in a story, they subtly persuade the reporter or re-write man to slant everything that follows so that it fits the stereotype. At best tiresome, and at worst misleading, such clichés form a trick that needs to be watched by the reader, listener or viewer. Is the person being described or quoted *really* as he or she is being represented? Or is there significant distortion hiding under a cliché?

The effect need not be denigratory. It can be the reverse. In some newspapers the clichés of 'heroes' and 'heroines', 'good Samaritans', 'good fairies' and so on, abound.

Sometimes these clichés may be justified (though even if they are justified, they would be better expressed in more original and precise words) but often they are plainly po-faced exaggeration. If the exaggeration were to be expressed in original language, its veracity might be questioned by readers; but because it is expressed in a comfortable, familiar cliché or clichés, it sails past the mind's defences without difficulty.

The words 'Make no mistake ...' at the beginning of a sentence is a cliché which has the effect of implying that no one could possibly contest what follows. Another such cliché is 'To be fair,' at the beginning of a sentence. This again implies that no one would be entitled to dispute what follows, when it is quite possible that what follows could be disputed legitimately on many grounds. 'Let's face it,' is a cliché which implies that anyone who does not accept the argument or slant of the journalist is somehow trying his best to escape incontestable facts.

Such examples of cliché that can bypass even a rigorous brain indicate how dangerous cliché can be in numbing the mind. There are many other examples of soothing phrases that say in effect, 'You really must believe this,' or, 'You really mustn't dispute this.'

They can be the journalist's version of the door-to-door salesman's soothing matiness when he is trying to sell a commodity or a service which in fact deserves rigorous and cool examination.

It is easy to patronize other people for allowing their vigilance to evaporate in the face of clichés. It is more difficult to ensure that, in your own case, different clichés – perhaps clichés more targeted to your own cast of mind – are an object of mistrust and maybe of deserved derision. Words and phrases like 'compassion', 'accessibility', 'elitism' and 'moving on' have become clichés. It may often be wise to question whether their use is precise and appropriate, or a convenient trick to make dubious, or at least controversial, actions more acceptable by the use of such comforting – because familiar – clichés.

One word that has become an almost meaningless cliché might even persuade opponents of the death penalty to change their minds. This is the word 'stunning' which, used repeatedly and wantonly as it is today, allows users to escape from having to think what they specifically mean. If you are hit round the side of the head with a shovel, that is stunning. If anything else has happened, a more precise word is required. If you see a flamboyant car go by, it may be flashy. If you hear Beethoven well played, it may be powerful. If you see a woman in a skimpy dress it may be revealing. But it is best to avoid 'stunning' as the adjective in such cases, and to avoid journalists who don't agree.

Clichés may be employed for their misleadingly soothing effect. But words can also be employed for provocative effect when they are put together to play with possibilities that have been posing too long as facts, rather than with facts themselves. What is involved could be called 'This is frightful – or perhaps it isn't' stories.

14

Wilful Ignorance

When Prince William was nineteen, one newspaper ran a front-page story saying 'it' could be Kenya's most controversial killing since the murder of Lord Erroll and the mysterious events which were made into the film *White Mischief*. Beside the story was a large colour picture of Prince William.

The story then posed the question, which was the essence of the 'it' in the story: did Prince William really shoot a protected Ibis bird during his gap-year safari in East Africa?

Even if Prince William *had* shot a protected bird, some readers might have considered that the story belonged on page 5 at best. Even in an era when the most trivial royal tittle-tattle is hyped as a matter of course into soap opera, page 1 seemed rather too ambitious.

The story went on to explain that the shooting occurred in the fading twilight in the Laikipia ranches, where Prince William had been tracking poachers, riding camels and helping to save rhinos. An African bush-tracker had shouted, 'Ndege', meaning bird, and Prince William had fired both barrels of his twelve-bore shotgun, thinking it was a game bird. Only in the last paragraph of the story was it revealed that the bird was probably a habada ibis, which was not an endangered species at all but a fairly common bird.

Undeterred, the following day another newspaper carried a front-page story with an intro saying that Prince William was at the centre of a murder mystery to rival the death of Cock Robin – before revealing, well down in the body of the story, that the bird was in fact regarded as little more than vermin.

The stories on successive days amounted to sleight of hand to conceal the fact that many people with robust good sense would say that the story was not in reality about anything very much. The trick lay in conjuring up vivid intros based on wilful, tactical, ignorance – of ignoring all the known facts in order to pose a dramatic question, and then burying deep in the story any facts that would undermine the drama in the intro of the story.

It was as if there was a story which began, 'Did the Prince steal a ladder from an old lady to get back into Buckingham Palace by climbing over a wall after a late night party yesterday?' and which contained only in the seventh paragraph the answer: 'No.' This has become a popular and accepted trick.

Some may think it can be defended as being merely a harmless dressing up of rumours to make them more exciting and entertaining: a mere piece of window dressing. Perhaps this may be so in the case of 'human interest' stories about royalty and other celebrities. But the principle that stories can be introduced on a skewed basis, and then inconspicuously straightened out later, is the thin end of a dangerous wedge. How soon before other, more serious, stories are treated in the same way? Even stories about the political intentions of governments and other power-brokers?

Some critics of journalists may suggest that this process is already happening and that political attitudes are effectively dramatized by using intros whose whipped-up drama is factually denied or undermined only well into the body of the story. It is a possibly pernicious trick which can be discouraged only by readers, listeners and viewers recognizing it, finding it increasingly irritating, and registering their disapproval in any way they can.

It may be a mistake to blame individual reporters for such a trick, or for that matter many other tricks, because no reporter can be an absolutely free agent. It may be that what is expected of him 'back at the office' is the dominating factor in what he writes, or at least in what he gets published.

15

The Feeling In the Office ...

A soldier who attempted to fight a battle entirely on the basis of step-by-step instructions fed to him from three or four thousand miles away via an earpiece would soon be captured or dead.

Do honest or would-be honest journalists sometimes find that their own version of a battle, or any other situation, is compromised because their interpretation of events comes not from themselves or other people with immediate knowledge of what is actually happening, but from power-brokers sitting in the office with only their own dogma, ego and career for guidance?

When he was appearing on the BBC's record-choice programme *Desert Island Discs* in July 2001, the former BBC international reporter Martin Bell, who became an anti-corruption Member of Parliament for Tatton for four years, pointed out that the widespread use of the mobile telephone had weakened the authority and integrity of the reporter on the spot by constantly feeding him the insidious line: 'The feeling in the office is that ...'

This cannot be dismissed as the prejudice of a lone maverick.

In his 2004 book *My Trade*, Andrew Marr, then BBC political editor, said it would be wrong to get too steamed up about the fact that modern news is affected by celebrity stories and sex stories. What concerned him more were the trends in British news values that were related to the growth of 'an office-based editorial culture, rather than a reporters' journalism'.

A great many skilled reporters, especially those trained in less conformist times, will agree enthusiastically with that diagnosis. The 'feeling in the office', the more dangerous because it is not visible to the public, should be subordinate to intelligence from the spot. In practice, it is sometimes not so subordinate. If there is a clash between the man on the spot and perceptions back in the office, the man on the spot almost certainly *should* win. But in practice this sometimes does not happen. Because the man on the spot is by definition not there in the office to assert his case forcefully face to face, he is too easily over-ruled.

What can happen is that the on-the-spot reporter becomes a puppet manipulated by head office, just as the studio interviewer or other broadcaster is manipulated by the producer breathing instructions or 'suggestions' into his ear via an earpiece. Of course, in the case of newspapers, the management may have their editorial line on issues of the day; but on matters of fact simple common sense surely must dictate that trust in the man on the spot is vital, especially if he has shown himself to be reliable.

Before the days of the mobile telephone, the on-the-spot reporter had his own remedy against interference. If he feared opposition from the office, he made sure that he was unreachable and took any necessary decisions that might be disputed back in the office without first telephoning. If he was covering an ecological disaster and thought it necessary to participate in the hiring of a helicopter to survey all the damage in a way that was possible only from the air, he would hire it and present the office with a fait accompli: a good story, and the bill. He would not have had to argue with accountants talking only the language of money.

With mobile telephones and plugged-in keyboards having become a fact of life, he can no longer do this. Now that accountants back at the office are often more powerful than journalists, on-the-spot journalists sometimes work on the basis of what is economically expedient rather than what is journalistically right.

The attempted influencing of the angle and tone of stories can be even more baleful, and it is arguable that here above all the best judge may be the man on the spot. An illustration of what can happen when there is happily no such office brow-beating may be drawn from my own experience. Before the 1964 general election I was a *Guardian* Midlands correspondent with my colleague Roger Silver. I was sent to cover the election campaign in one especially interesting constituency, Smethwick near Birmingham, which had a large number of immigrants. Fighting the seat for Labour was the sitting MP, the veteran Patrick Gordon-Walker, an honest and decent man who was expected to be Foreign Secretary if and when Harold Wilson's Labour Party won the election.

But leaflets had been circulating, reading 'If You Want a Nigger Neighbour, Vote Labour'. It was the first British election campaign in which race was an issue. The view in *The Guardian*'s head office, and indeed in many quarters of the media, was that the Conservatives were playing the race card and inventing social problems that were allegedly caused by immigrants, but that the decency of the electorate would be dismissive of that tactic.

Patrick Gordon-Walker's home was in Hampstead, and was described as a 'mansion' by the Conservatives who were eager to paint a picture of the difference between Smethwick, home of the industrial working class, and Hampstead, home of the intellectuals and the wealthy. The young and ambitious Conservative candidate Peter Griffiths was thought to be sympathetic to those in the constituency who had complaints against the behaviour of some ethnic groups, and were arguing that unless those complaints were faced and addressed by the principal political parties, as they were not being addressed by Labour, the voters would turn to extreme right-wing parties and possibly to violence.

The 'view in the office' might well have been that this was one hundred per cent untrue and opportunistic humbug, and that the sitting Labour MP Patrick Gordon-Walker was a blameless hero. After I arrived on the scene, I began to see the situation rather differently. Although I was sure that some supporters of the Conservative candidate were indeed playing the race card, I also came to the conclusion that part of the trouble was that the sitting MP, far from fighting the opposition head-on, had taken the position that anyone who did want to talk about race relations must be a racist, and had totally withdrawn from involvement in the whole subject, and into himself, in the hope that the problem would simply go away if it was not talked about.

The Conservatives suggested that women in some areas of the constituency were afraid to go out at night, or to answer their doors, an assertion for which they had been widely denounced by those on the political left. There had been suggestions of racial tensions in a certain street. The Labour Party formed a group of researchers to go round in the evening, knocking on doors to find out what if anything was really happening, and they invited me to go with them. They found that some householders were reluctant to open their doors, and that there were no women out in the street. When the researchers came to a house occupied by immigrants who did open the door, they discovered that the lady of the house was relieving herself in her back garden. They asked me to leave their group, but I declined. Some constituents had told me that they resented their MP because he gave the impression of brushing off as racist any complaints where an immigrant was involved. At this point, the researchers discontinued that evening's research.

One of the sitting member's public meetings was the most surreal, macabre and unpleasant meeting I have ever covered. I expected it to be packed with Labour supporters, and perhaps it was. But if so, they missed few opportunities to *boo and hiss* their candidate, sometimes driving him to silence while he stood there like a wounded stag, and his wife beside him looked composedly at the booers and hissers with steely and steady blue eyes. Perhaps she should have been handling the situation. He failed to receive any applause when he finally sat down. It was uncomfortably obvious that some, perhaps many, of his nominal supporters hated him. The unfortunate man had all too obviously drifted apart from the people who should have been supporting him; indeed, had alienated his own traditional supporters on a singular, massive and disastrous scale.

That man who had been expected to be Foreign Secretary in Harold Wilson's newly elected government lost the seat to the Conservatives, who held a noisy celebration at the declaration of the poll. I covered this event. I can still remember arriving home at three in the morning and putting Bach's Third Brandenburg Concerto on my record-player as a reminder that there could be some sanity in the world. Later that day I wrote a piece making clear my views on the outcome, and what had brought it about.

It would have been easy for me to follow the 'feeling in the office', which might have been inclined to look with unqualified favour on the distinguished Patrick Gordon-Walker. I had at the time been working for *The Guardian* only a matter of months. If I had been conventionally ambitious, or more supine, that is the line I would have been tempted to take. But greed or fear are poor sole motives for any course of action. Also, *The Guardian* had a long tradition of trusting the man on the spot, and it did not attempt in any way to censor what I saw and heard. The 'feeling in the office' was never invoked. But I confess to being relieved when certain Labour figures, local and national, told me – not publicly, of course – that they thought I had assessed the situation correctly.

The lesson here is that, for a newspaper which values its integrity, the 'feeling in the office' should only assert itself with caution in the face of facts delivered by the man on the spot. It is the man on the spot who creates valuable journalism, as journalists who have worked for organizations that have given them a substantially free rein would no doubt gladly testify.

It should be accepted that honest reporters – even though in general they do have to accept the philosophy of their paper if they are to be comfortable – will see what is there, which is not just what 'the feeling in the office' dictates. 'The feeling in the office', if it conflicts with the man on the spot, may amount to little more than a group of executives with important-sounding titles displaying self-importance and their ignorance of the facts on the ground, or else pandering to a dogmatic pro-prietor.

It must be remembered that reporters and correspondents are not always responsible for the things that are said, and not said, under their by-lines. If you come across an 'action' report that could have been written from the office on the basis of known existing prejudices, bear it in mind that the trick may have been that it *was,* at least in effect, written that way, the 'feeling in the office' having achieved far too much dominance for the good of the section of the media involved, or of the public.

Reporters have long become used to having things cut out of their stories. A newer phenomenon is having things *inserted* into their stories under their by-line, which can be a far more dangerous trick, especially if what is inserted conflicts in any way with the reporter's knowledge of what is in fact happen-ing at the scene of the action.

From the reader's point of view, one useful indicator of there being undue 'feeling in the office' is too obvious 'party-line-ing' in what is presented as a news report.

In the electronic media, there are guidelines about political balance. The dangers can be rather different. One of them is that when film shots of far-off places are available in the studio, the person the public considers to be the 'man on the spot' may sometimes not be the man on the spot at all, but someone who is making judgments from far away on the basis of the footage available in the studio.

16

Absentee Commentators

A television reporter can be made to 'see' on-the-spot things he has never seen, nor even got anywhere near. This is one of those journalistic tricks that prove that the camera can, and does in effect, lie.

To send a journalist to a trouble spot is expensive as well as being dangerous. There are his hotel bills, the high cost of hire cars, and the cost of possible help for the widow should he be killed. One can imagine the media accountants, who now dominate much of journalism, irritably working all this out and not liking the result.

Good journalism is all very well, one can almost hear them muttering, but it is money that is sacred! Why not keep our valuable journalists sitting in comfortable armchairs in the office the whole of the time? If that is too utopian, how much better it would be to use brief clips of dangerous trouble spots supplied by news agencies, and to have the 'on-the-spot' journalist talking to camera about what is being screened when he is in fact several hundreds or thousands of miles away, or even in the office.

What is wrong with that? Accountants may not be able to see what is wrong. Most journalists would, and so would members of the public if they knew exactly what was going on. What is wrong is that the viewer is receiving a flimsy or even false picture of what is actually happening. The journalist talking knowledgeably to camera may not have seen, or been anywhere near, the incidents portrayed in the clips and cannot, in such a case, be earning the usually justified reputation for authority that is generated by such pictures.

This is not mere carping on the part of a print journalist, who in any case may have his own version of the phenomenon – for example a story from a trouble spot under his by-line but with wodges of news agency material, or material from other sources, slotted into it without attribution.

In general, the days when eminent journalists could and did insist that their own work should not be cut, re-written or added to without consultation are over. A new Faustian pact has been struck: the journalist gets the glory of talking to camera if he is working for television, or of a large and imposing, if not entirely earned, by-line if he is working for print media.

The *Daily Mirror*'s great columnist of the war and postwar years, Cassandra (Sir William Connor), once went to cover a nuclear bomb test in the Pacific. Because of the time difference from London, the moment of the test was on the very edge of the deadline of all the British newspapers who were represented.

It was known roughly what the explosion would be like: the blinding flash, the expanding mushroom of smoke, the delayed searing blast, and so on. Some journalists, worried about the deadline, filed their stories of what had happened before it did, reporting speculation as fact. Connor refused to do this, and filed only on the basis of what he had actually seen and heard, so producing a different, superior column that was nonetheless too late for the first edition, which his professional rivals had made. The pugnacious Connor was criticized in the office for not having filed in advance. His comments are not known, but they were likely to have been incandescent.

Today it is not impossible to imagine that, in similar circumstances, a news desk might simply shovel in some rewritten and jazzed-up news agency material under a Cassandra-style by-line. That would be extreme, but the authority of the individual journalist in such a case has been shrunk to that of the supplier of 'product'; and in the absence of his 'product' his employers may simply import somebody else's 'product' and put his 'brand name' on it.

Such a trick, in print or on television, can assume the aura of a confidence trick. The habit of shovelling in material that obliquely or directly suggests that the journalist was there when he wasn't, might with benefit be replaced by a rule that the material of the man on the spot is, except in exceptional circumstances, virtually sacrosanct. Another utopian dream. But technological tricks are not to be excused merely because they are technically possible.

Nor are certain time-honoured, dishonoured, ritual demands and gestures that are often made by journalists, or by other people with their assistance (whatever the technology employed), necessarily free from tricks.

17

Apologize!

Stanley Baldwin, British Prime Minister in the 1930s, was once told by lawyers that an accusation levelled at him by a popular newspaper would entitle him to an apology and substantial damages. He replied that an apology from them would be of no value, and that he would not touch their money with a ten-foot pole.

Such a degree of moral scorn and financial disinterestedness may seem strange in our later era, when money has achieved the status of a religion. But, in treating the possibility of an apology with contempt, that particular Prime Minister had logic on his side. Of what value is an enforced apology in itself? Yet trying to extort one from any party to a disaster or scandal has become a popular journalistic trick whose entertainment role is presumably increasing and whose value is seldom questioned.

In reality, money has accelerated those calls for apologies because extracting an apology could be the first stage in setting up a lucrative legal action. Imagine that there has been a railway disaster in which many people have been killed or injured. Almost immediately the manager responsible for the track, for the locomotive or for the rolling stock is asked by newspaper, television or radio interviewers why he has not apologized for the incident. Relatives of the dead or injured have already been interviewed, and have pointed out that those responsible have not apologized. They imply that their grief would be lessened, that the absence of dead loved ones would be not so unbearable if some representative of 'those responsible' had mouthed the words, 'We are sorry; we apologize.' They are shown in the media as pining for justice when sometimes they may be pining for money. On occasion, therefore, an apology may be looked for as the first part of a campaign to get cash. That fact may have had the undesirable effect of lessening the chances of an apology of any sort being given, even in cases where money is not the main issue, or an issue at all.

So the interviewer repeatedly asks the man facing the microphone to utter an apology and derides his evasions. This may be thought to make excellent print, television or radio journalism. In fact it sometimes boils down to a journalistic trick to make a possibly complex situation more exciting and confrontational, enabling even the slower-witted 'consumers' to have something to argue about at home. 'Will he apologize or won't he? Ten to one against!'

If the person being interviewed says simply, 'Naturally we are sorry that people have been killed or injured,' he will be told that this is not the full apology for the accident that relatives and friends of the dead and injured want and need.

Plainly, the spokesman will not be prepared to go further at that point – but only if and when an official enquiry has attributed the blame to the organization he represents, by which time any apology may be considered to be emotionally, if not legally, redundant. Yet the journalist will often convey the implication, in his questions and remarks, that such a refusal is in some way suspect. And the spokesman will have no defence except to look serious and say that the matter is being thoroughly investigated.

In recent years we have seen how Authority of any kind reacts to the apology-hunt. First, it sets up some sort of official inquiry that will be so 'thorough' that it will be months before it reports. In the meantime Authority says that it would be improper to apologize or make any sort of statement until the inquiry has reported. In this way, silence is justified until the heat has gone out of the public reaction.

This trick played *against* journalists certainly justifies the media continuing with their own unofficial enquiries. But the simple trick of automatically pressing for an apology in the absence of any official inquiry, or in the absence of any relevant facts dug up by the media, provokes questions.

Is it journalism or is it an entertaining blood-sport? Is it a poor substitute for more specific questioning that would require more knowledge of the subject, more investigative and interrogative skills – which might produce more revealing answers?

At one level, an apology can be important. It can indicate

that a party is taking moral or legal responsibility for events and it may be a factor in deciding any legal or quasi-legal penalty. If the interviewer says, 'Do you accept responsibility?' that question (though it is unlikely to be answered frankly) may have a *directly* commercial value. Except in this context, the value of extracting an apology consisting of the specific words 'I/we are sorry' from anyone questioned, is doubtful. If a pedestrian has been killed by a car, of course the driver, if he is not a monster, is sorry. But whether he is therefore legally liable is quite another matter: it may have been mainly the pedestrian's fault.

An apology has become rather like a football in a game: a thing of little intrinsic value, but for which people are nevertheless willing to compete with every nerve in their bodies. No one in the middle of the match, either on the pitch or in the stands, ever asks himself, 'How intrinsically valuable is that football?' Similarly, fewer people seem to be asking themselves, 'What is the intrinsic value of the enforced apology this journalist is seeking – unless it is a trial by media in which legal penalties can be imposed? Does it really establish legal responsibility, or is it just a statement that one human being (or organization) is sorry for the sufferings of another? Does it bind a wound? Does it restore a dead man to his loved ones? Does it make the orphan no longer an orphan?'

Leave aside the issue of how far, if at all, the phrase 'I'm sorry' is a legal admission of guilt (and, in any case, it has been held that what appears in a newspaper report is not legal evidence) as distinct from a compassionate reaction to the misfortune of another human being.

The only apology of *emotional* value, in private or public life, is one given voluntarily, sincerely and preferably immediately. That may restore human relations between the parties to a tolerably decent level. In strenuously fishing and tussling for the uttering of cliché words of apology, intelligent journalists must sometimes suspect that they are indeed participating in a dramatic trick that has more entertainment value than moral or social value.

Trying to provoke apologies when the rights and wrongs are dubious is a trick which in practice implies that human beings do not exist in shades of grey but are either wholly good or wholly bad – heroes or villains. Which brings us to another journalistic trick of over-simplification.

18

Heroes and Villains

Turning human beings into 'heroes' and 'villains' may be thought a harmless journalistic trick to create colour and excitement, and so liven up their readers', listeners' or viewers' dull grey lives. Heroes and villains appear mostly in tabloid newspapers, and in the more vacuous magazines, rather than in the broadsheets and the electronic media, although a novelettish attitude to life may now obtrude in all varieties of media.

A few fictitious examples will clearly illustrate the syndrome. 'My Hero Husband Catches Burglars'. 'Schoolboy Hero Defies Bullies'. 'Heroine Chases Runaway Horse'. 'Heroine Fights Cancer'. 'Hero Fights Muggers'. Or, on the contrary: 'Welfare Payments Villain Caught'. 'Evil Scrounger's Life of Luxury Unmasked'. 'Love Rat Exposed'. 'My Rat Husband Gave Me No Housekeeping While He Screwed Model'.

Is this trick of forcing real people into categories of heroism and villainy quite as harmless as might at first be thought? The danger is that human judgment will be coarsened, and that those who come to believe in such a melodramatic categorization will tend to begin to put the real people in their *own* lives into these arbitrary boxes. In fact, people who deserve the description hero or villain are few and far between: most people are fallible human beings who behave well on some occasions and less well in other situations.

For a journalist to paint human beings in extreme shades may sometimes be justified – or at least expected of him by his employers. But the temptation must be this: that if there is no obvious villain or hero around today, the journalist will have to create one. The result can be that too much is heaped upon the shoulders of an actress no one has heard of until her ex-boyfriend informs on her for heavy drinking and domestic violence, and too much sanctity is attributed to the refuse collector who finds a wallet containing £500 in his front garden and hands it in to the police.

Is the actress really a villain, and is the refuse collector really a hero? Or is the actress a human being who is sadly out of kilter and needs help rather than betrayal, and the refuse collector simply the honest man he and everybody else should be? It is the refusal to see mitigating or qualifying circumstances before creating a hero or villain that distorts what human beings are really like, and makes it easier for readers to indulge in name-calling rather than human understanding in their own lives.

There are certainly some nasty people about who may have done nothing that would enable the law to deal with them, but nevertheless deserve to be exposed. Various television and radio series have exposed tradesmen who take large sums of money and then don't provide the new utility-room extensions or outhouses promised, or provide grossly sub-standard ones. Such programmes do a useful job in warning the public against shysters whom the police might find it difficult to prosecute.

This is worthwhile journalism which does not rely on melodramatic name-calling but gives facts to show that a particular individual is best avoided. To call the individual concerned a 'swine', a 'rat' or even a 'barmy builder' adds nothing to the valuable chronicle of unpalatable facts.

That great *Manchester Guardian* editor C. P. Scott memorably said that facts are sacred, comment is free. He also said that it was well to be frank, better to be fair. In the present context, it is easy to imagine him saying that facts are sacred, but terms of abuse or adulation should be used with moderation and discretion if they are not to amount to a lurid and coarsening trick.

Not the least of the penalties for too profligate a use of 'heroes', 'villains', 'rats' and other novelettish labels is that when there really *is* a hero (for example, a man or woman who, knowing the risks, gives a kidney to an afflicted loved one or friend) or a villain (for example, a murderous paedophile), all the appropriate terms have exhausted their potential impact through over-use.

The trick of calling too many people by such novelettish good or bad names in the end cheapens them rather than en-hances or demolishes them. It contributes to the sorry con-temporary tendency of treating words not as priceless tools of exact expression but as modish wallpaper. It is a tendency that belittles us all.

There is another trick in the deployment of words which seeks dramatic effect at the cost of civilized perception, and which also deserves appraisal.

19

Rudeness

Rudeness is sometimes used by journalists as a substitute for wit. It requires less thought and intellectual discrimination – and any fool should be able to understand it.

The trouble usually occurs in feature articles, opinion columns and reviews rather than news stories, although it is not unknown there: fashions tend to spread. It is so much easier to describe an opera singer as a 'tub of lard' than to think out a more relevant and fair opinion. 'She looks as if her life is one long, self-indulgent uninterrupted meal, and her voice and manner match her appetite and her looks' might at least show that the journalist deserved a pat on the back for trying to be witty. It might be considered more pointed, funny and evocative than the merely rude throwaway phrase (which also now happens to be a cliché): 'tub of lard'.

People who have disputes in the columns of newspapers are often not as polite as George Bernard Shaw and G. K. Chester-ton would have been in the Edwardian and George V eras. One believed in the Life Force, the other in God. One was a tee-totaller, the other thought cocoa a social solecism. One was a Marxist who was lukewarm about Britain's part in the first world war, the other romanticized the British nation. But each respected the other, and their respect showed in the way they debated with civility, set on demolishing an *opinion* not a *person*.

But politeness even in disagreement is no longer common currency: not for perpetrators of controversial actions like politicians, nor for spectators like journalists, especially headline writers. In the London *Evening Standard* of 16 August 2001, at a time when the Conservative Party was looking for a new leader, a piece by the readable and entertaining columnist Matthew Norman on the politician Michael Ancram (a man, incidentally, of invariable politeness) was headed: 'A great pudding of a statesman'. The text tried to justify the heading, arguing that Iain Duncan Smith was 'a third rate no-hoper who will lead the Tories directly to oblivion', but would nevertheless be preferable as Conservative Party leader to 'a grubby careerist posing as a man of principle like that pudgy puffball Michael Ancram'. At least one reader and respecter of the combative columnist reflected that the attack on Ancram might have been more telling if it had been more elegantly descriptive of his personality, opinions and ambitions and not merely so rude. But the columnist was not far out of step with contemporary controversy techniques.

In the current atmosphere, which often resembles that rough pub at closing time, when insults, belches and farts seem to be as acceptable forms of communication as shafts of perception and wit, it almost escapes notice that newspapers have made a small but significant contribution to gracelessness by altering their polite practice of describing people by their titles: Lord Smith of Billericay, Sir John Smith, Mr John Smith, Mrs John Smith or Miss Joan Smith.

This may be a less trivial point than it might at first appear. Fifty years ago there was a polite convention that people mentioned in newspapers – whether politicians giving their views in the news columns or actors mentioned in critiques – were always Mr, Mrs, or Miss. Mr Smith may have given, in the opinion of a critic, a sub-standard performance in George Bernard Shaw's *Candida*, but he remained Mr Smith, and the author of the play, even if it were not the critic's favourite Shaw play, remained Mr Shaw.

There was one exception to this rigorous politeness in address, and that was when Mr John Smith was a defendant in a case at a magistrate's court, or higher court, when he suddenly became plain John Smith. The loss of the polite use of the title Mr was thought to be a deterrent to having any involvement with the courts as a defendant: guilty or innocent, respectability had been impugned by the mere proximity of Mr Smith to a court of law.

The contrast with the present day could not be more marked. Prime Ministers are written of as Thatcher, Major, Blair and so on, while on a different page of the same newspaper even an alleged serial killer in court may be accorded the title of Mr, as if the newspaper were straining to be 'democratic' and 'enlightened'. Is this anything other than perverse? It may be argued that in taking the position of denying decent people the dignity of their title, whatever it may be, journalists are merely reflecting the attitude of society as a whole. It is also arguable that they are not only reflecting it: they are encouraging it.

It is not for nothing that for hundreds of years Members of Parliament, however disputatious, and however contemptuous of those members on the facing benches, have addressed each other as 'the Honourable Member for Wherever' and not as 'Smith!' as if reproving an incompetent waiter or valet. This is a polite device whose aim is to encourage members to cover up their animosities in polite forms of speech. There is now a thread of opinion among many people, including journalists, which holds that polite ways of address are somehow 'hypocritical', whereas unpleasant forms of address are somehow 'sincere'. This is surely too pessimistic a view of what human beings are 'really' like. It would be truer to say that they can in fact be encouraged to act well or to act badly, and avoiding rudeness, and clearly showing respect for other people, are two of the ways people can behave better.

When journalists, sometimes as prisoners of an editorial policy decided above their heads, adopt the trick of reducing the dignity of others by referring to them not as Mr Smith or Lord Smith, but almost as if they were mere numbers in a Victorian prison rather than free human beings – especially while inflating their own dignity and egos, whenever and wherever possible – they are not living up to their full potential as influential and productive members of the community.

Rudeness in journalism (and that habit of not according to human beings the dignity of their title, which may be thought of as a form of rudeness) is a wasting asset, if asset it can ever be called. Having called a minister 'a cross-eyed slug who has shat on the electorate for years', how is the argument to be developed by taking the rudeness further? By calling him a *huge* cross-eyed slug?

Rudeness has two practical advantages, one to the perpetrator of the rudeness and one to the recipient. It is one thing the most dodgy politician can shrug off, since it amounts to vulgar abuse rather than libel. And the perpetrator of mere vulgar abuse is less likely to be sued than the perpetrator of a specific libel, about a target's financial affairs, for example, and less likely to be awarded a large sum in damages. If there is one thing a money-man-led industry dislikes, it is paying large sums in damages. Far cheaper to adopt the trick of drawing rude attention to the attacked one's large red nose, fatness, thinness, baldness or eyes set too closely together, however limited a relevance to a man's professional performance and status these attributes may have.

Management penny-pinching has a relevance in other areas. It has led in some quarters to the virtual extinction of that vital servant of the journalism industry, the so-called proof-reader, or his electronic counterpart.

20

To Be Fare ...

Not all journalistic tricks, or what the public may see as journalistic shortcomings, are the responsibility of journalists themselves. Some are forced on them by those money-conscious proprietors and their accountants, or by outside circumstances over which they have little control, and of which the public may have little or no awareness.

One of the most noticeable effects of the penny-pinching trick, especially in the local and regional press, is the failure to provide them with enough cash to cover the cost of adequate proof-reading or page-checking, so that irritating lapses in spelling, grammar and, more significantly, *meaning*, too readily occur – to say nothing of simple typing mistakes.

Everything that goes into a newspaper or magazine should be checked word for word by men and woman skilled in this operation. Though digital and photographic processes may have usurped old-fashioned printing techniques, checking every word that appears remains a duty, and it is often one that is in-adequately performed.

Here are some examples of what faces the reader when that happens. They are from one issue of a local paper, which will not be named because I do not wish to imply that it is unique in its blundering.

'The X, a 13-storey office tower, faced sterne (*sic*) criticism from councillors and residents when it was first put forward last Janu-ary.' [Did the paper perchance mean the distinguished writer Sterne?]

'Y—Z—, who is heading the campaign, supported the coun-cils (*sic*) move to serve local notices ...' [The careless placing of apostrophes is now endemic. It should, of course, have been 'council's'.]

'I am really pleased that the council is taking it's (*sic*) job seri-ously. I am very happy about that.' [Another misbehaving apostrophe. It should have been 'taking its job seriously'. 'It's' is a contraction of 'it is', not a possessive.]

In a previous issue, a building was 'raised (*sic*) to the ground' by builders. This is something that could happen only to a cellar: what was meant was obviously 'razed'.

In a subsequent issue, these gaffes occurred:

'A planned Controlled Parking Zone extension in X has been

delayed following a area committee meeting.' ['An meeting' or 'an fiasco', or 'a enervating experience', one wonders? All publications should be able to tell their 'a's from their 'an's.]

'Roads in the proposed expansion comprise of ...' ['Comprise' means 'consist of'. Saying 'comprise of' is like saying, 'consist of of'.]

'... but this year we got more tickts (*sic*) so a dozen us were there.' [Missing a letter out of the word 'tickets' may be trivial, but missing out the 'of' in the phrase 'so a dozen of us' is more disorientating for the reader.]

'... but hopefully, as it was early in the morning that wouldn't have effected (*sic*) too many people.' [It wouldn't have *affected* too many people either. If you shouted abuse at someone, you would affect him. If he then hit you, you would have caused that effect.]

'Stopped in the street by police, a youth started waving a meat cleaver at them and had to be overpowered by a truncheon and CS gas.' [Clever robot truncheon and robot CS gas! Being able to act on their own, they are obviously the sort of weapons against crime which will tip the balance heavily in favour of the police. On the other hand, the intro probably meant, '... overpowered *with* a truncheon and CS gas.']

And so on.

But errors of this sort are not confined to local newspapers. One national newspaper, at roughly the same time as these local transgressions, quoted someone as saying that someone else 'had an adversity' to something or other. One could only hope that the person never had to face the challenge of a formidable aversion.

One of the dangers of journalism as a highly self-hyping activity is that more and more attention is given to award-winning, award-winners and other promotional tools, and less to the minutiae of the actual job. This preference for glamour over competence bears a stiff price.

It is time that what is about to appear in newspapers, or any other publications, was thoroughly read and corrected by educated professionals who know what they are doing, and keep their heads even when deadlines become pressing. Journalism should not be seen as giving support to the alarming trend towards greater illiteracy among the population as a whole. And journalists who will not mention the literal and other errors of other journalists because they fear they may make some themselves, or have some thrust on them by the re-write man, might with benefit screw up their courage and speak out to their masters and if necessary to the public. That would be a useful trick – and one that I hope I am perpetrating.

And mention of the re-write man brings us to the subject of sub-editors and what their tricks can contribute to the excellence or otherwise of journalism.

21

The Sub's Role

Every reporter 'knows' that a sub-editor correcting and editing his copy is merely a reporter who lacked the personality and persistence to carry out a job that involves meeting the public. Similarly, every sub 'knows' that he could have written any story he is subbing better than the reporter who has in fact written it.

This psychodrama with its consequent tricks is played out every day in the offices of newspapers, news agencies and magazines, sometimes to the detriment of all parties, including the reader. Under cover of having to reduce the length of a piece, the sub may not only cut but also re-write: in 'serving the interests of brevity' he may remove all qualifying phrases and statements, or eliminate necessary background and colour without which the facts, no longer being in context, cannot be correctly or fully understood. After this, perhaps perceiving a gap, he may insert some of his own phrases to fill it.

We know that too many cooks spoil the broth. The same can apply to the subbing of a story. Just because the reporter's name is at the head of a story does not mean that *he* has missed the point of it: that failure could be the sub's. Even leaving aside the dangers of re-writing, deletions entail a certain element of risk in themselves. If there is a passing reference in the original story to a person being tried for indecent exposure, and acquitted, it is absolutely vital to save the reference to the acquittal. This point is so obvious that the dimmest sub would feel compelled to follow it. There would be legal risks – notably of libel – if he did not.

But when the point is not a legal one but more about human relationships, mistakes may occur when any qualifying material is taken out. It would be extremely dangerous, in subbing an interview with an actress, to allow through the statement that she left her six-year-old child behind in Britain to go to Hollywood, while cutting out the qualifying information that her husband was between engagements and was able to look after the child, who had joined her in California after six days.

Some complaints by the public about 'unfair reporting' may rest on what has been done to the story after it has left the writer's hands. There may be some reporters who do not set much store by fairness; but, in the main, a writer in print journalism knows that his future access to people depends to a degree on his reputation for fairness. The sub is under no such restraint. He can sub without risk of alienating contacts a story in which an actress is quoted as saying she wears no knickers, cutting out her explanation that her doctor has suggested it to prevent the inflammation of an over-sensitive skin.

The subtler the point being made by the writer, the greater are the chances of it being lost in the subbing.

As a fictitious case, let us assume that a journalist is doing an interview or profile of an actor, Cedric Blandford, who is known to have had drinking problems. These started when he was starring in a regular comedy series on television in which he played the hard-drinking plumber Bert Plimsole, whose interventions when tight often had householders hilariously wishing they had never called him.

The actor himself started off without a drinking problem; indeed he drank little except an occasional glass of fine claret. The part he was playing was so popular, however, that strangers in the street would hail him not as Cedric but as 'Bert' and strangers in the pub would insist that 'Bert' had a pint on them. If he went on holiday to a seaside resort and a conference of, let us say, boilermakers was taking place, its members would soon insist on buying 'Bert' so many pints of beer that he would forget what time and what day it was. Soon, cursing the part he was playing, he had a drink problem of his very own.

In making this train of events intelligible to the reader, it would be essential not merely to say that people were always intrusively offering him drinks it would have been rude to his fans to refuse. Anyone, on rare occasions, might have been offered drinks which it would have been politic, on health grounds, to refuse. The essential point here would be that the people offering him drinks were offering them rapidly, thinking that would please the fictitious boozy 'Bert', in a way that they would never have offered them to Cedric Blandford, actor and lover of the occasional glass of fine claret. The actor was in effect martyred by the part he was playing, and by the public's reaction to it, because the part he was playing was quite unlike his true dignified self, and opened him up to misguided hospitality.

If it was not made clear that they were offering the fast-flowing drinks to 'Bert Plimsole', the irony of the situation would be lost, and the actor would be reduced to the status of just another human being blaming other people for his failings. A sub who removed the explanation for the offers of abundant drink originally contained in the story, would be culpable. And, in a sense, he would be misleading the public while safely hiding beneath another man's by-line.

The more occasional *insertion* of additional 'facts' by the sub may be justified if those facts prove to be accurate, though if too many such insertions are made, it means that stories are being shaped by the man in the office rather than the man on the spot. Sometimes the 'facts' thus introduced are not accurate: if they had been, perhaps the man on the spot would have included them himself. In such cases, the public is being short-changed of useful information, and given useless information, and all under the cover of another man's name.

It pays, if you seek to dodge such tricks, to read every story with great care, bearing in mind two possibilities. The introduction of 'facts' by the office rather than the front line may betray itself by standing out a little uncomfortably from the surrounding text. And the hand that has deleted necessary background material may have left in place faint but, to the alert eye, significant indications of what the central point of that background could have been.

These are two frail hopes, but they are better than nothing. The reader, like the reporter, should bear in mind that though good sub-editors are valuable people who head off mistakes and disasters while retaining the essence of a writer's copy, there *are* sometimes other people at work.

Although he himself may occasionally suffer from subbing, the drama or film critic, or the critic of any art, has quite different difficulties with self-expression, only one of them being that he may find it a necessary trick to write his review while the play or film is still in progress. The critic's main trick, certainly if he is a man of integrity, is to hide the fact as best he can that he can never be *completely* like other people in the audience for whom the play or film was fashioned – for one simple but often forgotten reason.

22

Critics

Professional critics, however conscientious, inevitably write from a skewed perspective. The reader, listener or viewer should always understand that fact.

The perspective is skewed because the critic knows that at the end of the show or book – or well before the end – he will have to *write something*, which is not something the average member of any audience will have to face. It is rather as if he went into an act of love knowing that he would be expected to write 600 words about it directly afterwards. A certain self-consciousness, among other possible effects, would be difficult to avoid.

The critic may as the result of his job tend unconsciously to think about his own journalism more than the playwright's play. This may lead him to be enthusiastic on the one hand, or vitriolic on the other, about productions he can use to write entertaining journalism rather than ones that are merely sound but offer him little scope for striking journalism. A smash hit or a maladroit turkey can be more welcome than something that is merely good of its type. This can produce a hair-trigger set of mind, where inequalities and deficiencies are attacked with a zeal that can be out of scale with the feelings of the rest of the audience.

The benevolent trick of professional critics is to put that fact to one side as far as possible. But the critic can never be in precisely the same position as a member of the audience who sees the show, has a drink and a chat in the interval and then goes home, perhaps – or perhaps not – discussing it with the people who saw it with him.

Not all critics can manage the trick of putting aside their special position, and not all try. Sometimes it shows and the reader is tempted to say: 'This critic has sat in the stalls for too long, and should get out more.'

That playwright and wit George Bernard Shaw said that his early period as a theatre critic had nearly killed him, and there may well be a case (though it would be massively resisted) for all professional critics having 'tours' in the job of no more than, say, three years, broken up by other work – such as covering courts or chasing ambulances for news stories. If the critic is not a eunuchoid personality who is perfectly content year after year to sit watching other people's work without wanting to get on with his own, he is apt to get impatient with what he is viewing after three or so years. This may be what happened to Shaw, *The Observer*'s Kenneth Tynan and other critics with ambitions on the other side of the footlights.

Even if he has no such ambitions, the task of criticizing live performances in particular can create hidden strains which can be unfair to all concerned. While I was in regional journalism, I had two periods as a theatre critic, for two different newspapers. Both periods lasted three years, at the end of each of which I was banned from the principal theatre because of my stringent reviews; and I could not bring myself to contest the bans, correctly deciding to move on and up. Looking back, I can see that I was always looking for an overwhelming experience to report and was secretly (but evidently not completely secretly) *too* underwhelmed when I didn't have one. Readers of critics should always bear it in mind that a lover's disappointment can generate more severity than an indifferent person's apathy.

That was all a long time ago. My youthful severity would be more appropriate now. We live in an age in which much that appears at the bookseller's, on the stage and on the big and the small screen is froth or trash unworthy of a critic's time – the sort of thing the critic might not choose to attend or pay any attention to as a private individual. And yet the individual critic is aware that if he too often, or ever, said, 'This is not worth reviewing, so I shall not review it,' a younger and less scrupulous critic would soon worm his way into doing the job. There is also the point that the public has a right to be advised on whether something is froth or trash or not, irrespective of the strain it may put on the critic who has more intelligence than the work under review.

When one distinguished and perceptive film critic wrote an article (or cry from the heart) entitled 'Why there's nothing to see at the cinema', however, it did show clearly the nature of the problem – and that critics do indeed suffer and struggle because of it. An entertaining television critic's lengthy ridicule of flea-brained television programmes, which might be essentially a waste of his and an intelligent audience's time, would be likely to confirm this.

The fact is that critics tend to be intelligent, and they need to be intelligent, whereas most of what would previously have been potential works of art directed at people of all levels of intelligence can now be no more than marketing-man-led froth or trash that is cynically directed at the *un*intelligent – as they are thought to be the more numerous sector of the paying public.

A critic faced with this situation can do one of two things, and the reader, listener or viewer should constantly bear this in mind when assimilating what he writes. He can cynically lower his standards to those of the providers of the froth and trash, or he can persist in (justified but increasingly wearing) vituperation against them until it becomes an encrusted mannerism and he becomes a caricature of that famous writer of letters under a nom de plume, Disgusted of Tunbridge Wells.

Neither outcome is satisfactory from the point of view of the public. If a critic lowers his standards and calls froth or trash acceptable because he thinks most of his moronic readers will agree with him, he will alienate intelligent opinion which, after one dire disappointment, will in future ignore anything he says.

If he constantly reviews at length a television programme that can produce combative journalism because it is trash, when he could be trying to find something to praise, the intelligent reader may in the end say, 'Why am I wasting my time reading about what this man says is trash, and why is he constantly wasting *his* time by talking about programmes which are a waste of time for everyone?'

In the latter case, there is a further danger. If the critic zealously ploughs through rubbish, even if in order to ridicule it, he may well end up by over-praising a programme, play or book merely for the lukewarm reason that it is *not* trash. It may catch him so much by surprise that his critical faculties sag in humble gratitude.

Either this, or his ridicule becomes a case of mental arthritis and he stiffly applies it to almost anything that comes his way, including works that deserve a spontaneous reaction rather than an arthritic one.

Undoubtedly much, though not all, modern art may be dismissed as trash that is palmed off on gullible art galleries and the public by untalented charlatans, chancers and exhibitionists who know how to play the media game. The fact remains that constant denunciation of them, in the absence of anything to praise, will in the end transform the critic into a bore and perhaps induce him to revise his standards downwards, or to become even more emphatic in his denunciations. He may come to rejoice in his status as a lone voice in the wilderness, a ruthless weeder-out of cant, and be tempted to adopt more extreme positions of hostility than fairness would justify.

To be a critic is now possibly to be sated with rubbish that is simply aimed at a different audience from the past: to be intelligent among the unintelligent. It may be argued by some that on the whole newspaper and magazine readerships get the critics they deserve: that broadsheet newspaper critics are intelligent and write for intelligent people, whereas tabloid newspaper critics are unintelligent and write for unintelligent readers – and why not?

But critics for unintelligent readers are not necessarily unintelligent themselves; they are adopting the trick of taking a stance that suits and entertains their readers, or that they think will do so. The accuracy of their artistic judgment is therefore at one step removed. They are continually asking themselves the question, 'What will the readers think?' rather than what it should have been, because it is more likely to lead to the expression of truth: 'What do I think?'

Such are among the difficulties which face critics in any era, and which face them specifically in this one. It might be claimed that a declining civilization tends to produce artistic trash in line with its own putrescence. If this is true, does the generalization fit our own era? And how much are critical perspectives and tricks of expression by critics affected? These are questions that may have to be asked about any criticism the reader, listener or viewer finds perplexing.

Critics deal with art rather than life, although the two should not be too far separated. When dealing with life itself, the desire for the dramatic, the colourful and the visceral may distort the perspective of journalists, journalists' financial bosses and journalism itself.

23

A Scandal or Not?

Scandal and disaster have always been news. The difference between other epochs and this one is that it is now assumed that nothing can really be news *unless* it is a scandal

Simply 'telling it as it is' has largely gone o
The role of the journalist as a perceptive and det
has been minimized while his role as entertai
levels of sophistication has been maximized, so
sometimes more closely resembles a disaster movie, or a pornographic video. The whim of the moment is often to revel in dirt
of all kinds for its own sake rather than for the sake of the
socially healthy exposure of the crooked and seedy.

There are some journalists who argue that, because politicians and other people with power have grown skilled at
burying as much bad news as possible – by putting it in boring-
looking, long items on the internet, or by introducing a minor
mess-up to distract attention from a major one, and so on – the
journalist is morally entitled to 'fix up' any man or woman of
power if he can do so. This is like saying that meeting a liar
entitles you to lie, or encountering a thief entitles you to steal.

Most newspapers who considered themselves responsible
used broadly to report the news as it happened, stage by stage.
If an organization announced its plans for some course of
action, these would be covered accurately, any comment being
confined to the leader columns. The next day, critics of the
plans would have mobilized and would have been reported
as having counter plans, which would be reported, comment
being confined once more to the leader columns.

From time to time, it happened that opposing groups were
telephoned and asked for a comment on the same day as the
announcement of a plan or policy; but such criticisms were
probably reported accurately a few paragraphs into the story,
or at the end of it, rather than in the intro.

In the 1980s, the Thatcherite emphasis on business competition helped to introduce the different atmosphere in which
news was reported. At its most obviously commercial level,
news was seen as a commercial commodity like any other. It
was more and more often referred to as a 'product', which had
to be 'improved', like a sausage or a motor car, to make it more
appealing to the reader than the 'products' of other organizations. In practice, this meant that a straight report of what was
happening, or what was being said, even if couched in punchy

words and short sentences, was no longer regarded as having sufficient pulling power. Whatever plans were announced had to be transformed into a potential disaster even before the reader had had a chance to familiarize himself with what was being proposed. Any achievement had to be shown to be less substantial than might commonly be supposed. Any mistake or aberration on the part of a public figure had to be a scandal.

In each of these, the way the facts were presented, and the tone of the writing, had to suggest disaster or scandal – something not quite right – even if reading the story to the end plainly indicated that the material showed nothing of the kind.

From being a phenomenon that had to be reported when it happened, disaster or duplicity had to be the content of almost *every* story. The fact that journalists were not the favourite people of Margaret Thatcher gave them an added incentive to wave the wand of show business's entertainment skills over their downbeat knocking stories. When a New Labour government came into power in 1997 it was eventually, after the honeymoon, an easy target because proprietors had a conditioned reflex to attack a supposedly left-wing government; and left-wing journalists had an equal compulsion to attack it on the grounds that it was not sufficiently left-wing.

These were the political factors at work. But the dominant factor was arguably that proprietors wanted plenty of sensational stories to compete with those of business rivals, and that they were not too fastidious about insisting that intros to stories should be fact-based rather than speculation-based. At the same time, some journalists themselves began to see 'professionalism' as having only an 'investigatory' role, the boring old business of 'telling it as it is' being quite passé, or even cravenly sycophantic. One well known television interviewer, Jeremy Paxman, said publicly that when he listened to any politician, he wondered why the bastard was lying. Is such an attitude merely the other side of the same coin – giving everyone a fair crack of the whip being replaced by giving *no one* a fair crack of the whip?

In print journalism, the same attitude tends to skew the introductory paragraphs of stories. It was in the 1980s, as those who then had contacts in Fleet Street were apt to observe when comparing notes, that news desks, when presented with a straight story about some organization, tended to ask, 'Yes, but where's the *real* story?' Stories had a better chance of prominence if they rubbished a plan or initiative from the start, even if it meant introducing speculative material into an intro, so that what was being reported was shown as irredeemably scandalous, vulnerable or disastrous.

No doubt the attraction of such an approach was partly dictated by Britain's new status as a 'can't do' society, as distinct from the American 'can do' society, which made attacking almost any project or person fit in with the 'can't do' public mood. As if to substantiate and underline the point, America is often credited with having more sober and straightforward journalism than contemporary Britain does.

But premature cries of 'Woe!' also became acceptable as a result of the gradual absorption of show business values into journalism, a story being regarded as a good story only if it was good as a piece of entertainment, however shaky the facts, and however stretched the speculation.

The fact that stories could and can be made entertaining *without* speculation, distortion or the manufacture of scandal seems largely to have been overlooked or else to have been pushed to the back of some journalists' minds. The art of achieving readability without distortion or vulgarity is on the wane, while the aggressive moulding of facts to give them more status as proof of scandal or disaster apparently thrives.

If it is considered as basically an honest craft with great social value, some contemporary journalism may thus be compromised. Even if it is considered as an inanimate industrial 'product', might not the same degree of quality control as would be exercised in the case, say, of motor cars, refrigerators or other mechanical 'products' conceivably be valuable?

Such quality control might well be exercised over the use of journalistic sources, too – identified, unidentified, or even perhaps invented, for good as well as for more questionable reasons.

24

Sources and Work

Honest reporting in the form of news stories is at the core of a journalist's value to the public. But there are a number of legitimate variations on news stories, notably feature articles and leading articles. What sort of trick is being played when you read, in newspapers and periodicals, pieces that are not quite news stories with unbiased, hard new facts, not quite features (articles that discuss a subject at length on the basis of new research) and not quite leading articles (expressions of corporate opinion)?

The journalist's trick is lazily to put out of his mind the notion that a journalist should be essentially an enquirer, not a day-dreamer. His craft should keep him active in the outside world, not trapped within his own intellectual processes, on his computer or in his cuttings file. It should keep him consulting plenty of separate *human* sources until he is in a position either to present some new facts in defence of an opinion, or to fashion existing facts into a feature that can present new conclusions.

Either will involve a process: sources first, conclusions second. There is nothing wrong with what used to be called a 'think piece', a piece of opinionated writing usually linked to a current news event, though not necessarily including any first-hand reporting. In local and regional journalism, think pieces were usually assignments given to the brightest and newest junior reporter, who wasn't yet ready to cover the County Court, let alone the Assizes, on his own. They came cheap and were considered to be part of the entertaining froth of journalistic life, not its centre.

The modern stars of journalism are producers of this sort of material at greater length, with their personal photograph (usually showing an attractive face rather than a thinking one) at the top of their column, and with salaries or fees that would make most working journalists believe they were in a different world – as, indeed, in a sense they are. They are in the world of show business rather than journalism. If their work shows intelligence, that can be considered a bonus.

The trick can be played, with less excuse, by interviewers as well as by columnists. It is possible in the electronics age to consult what cuttings are easily available and shovel the contents directly into the 'new' interview, along with anything else that can be found on websites and the internet. In this way, the same old facts and quotes can be recycled to make up much or most of the interview, provided that it is then garnished with new turns of phrase and personal impressions and opinions.

A better trick, especially if the subject of an interview is of some stature, is for the journalist to have an empty notebook, fill it with genuinely new material that is gained in the course of the interview, and then present it in such a way that he does not get in the way of, and obscure, the subject. An historical example may indicate that the modern trick of not applying any restraint at all, except the law of libel, to pushy opinions is not necessarily progress when compared with some journalism of the nineteenth century.

In *The Daily Telegraph* of 10 and 11 June 1890, the Prussian statesman Bismarck was interviewed by William Beatty-Kingston (the interview was reproduced in the *Penguin Book of Interviews*, edited by Christopher Silvester, and published in 1993). He adopted a technique that might well be sneered at today. In effect, it was that of a patient, respectful local-newspaper reporter interviewing the great statesman and would-be unifier of Europe as they both walked around the forests Bismarck had planted for posterity – Bismarck commenting on the forests, saying why he had created them and what they meant to him, and expressing himself on public affairs generally, as he strode along, or stopped to recharge and light his pipe. For a reader in the twenty-first century, the magical effect is that of meeting a legend face to face, in an interview devoid of affectation from Bismarck or the man who was talking to him.

Suppose it had been done with the use of some contemporary journalism's tricks, for instance with the interjection of the interviewer's personal impressions and reactions rather than of concrete facts, or the insertion of clever or clever-clever remarks. The interviewer would in effect have stood in front of Bismarck, preventing us from seeing him or hearing him. An intelligent reader might have wished to strangle the obtrusive clever-clogs. And suppose that the interview had been done by some contemporary journalist who appeared to think – perhaps because they went to the same school or university – that their own reflections were of equal or superior weight to those of the person being interviewed. If that were really the case, why would he, or his organization, have bothered to interview the person concerned, except to show the interviewee in a poor light?

Finding sources of real value to the public in news stories or features usually demands patience and work. The amount of patience and work that is applied (or the level of trickery to hide the fact that not much work has been done) may well establish the true value of the piece.

A journalist should at least first listen to his sources, and not to sounds in his own head. However gratifying to his sense of personal importance those sounds may be, they will almost inevitably result in inferior journalism. The only likely exception is when the journalist is reporting on some unusual experience he has had *personally*. If he has lost his family in a terrorist attack, has been locked up in some dictator's filthy prison for reporting all too accurately what is going on in his country, has won ten million pounds on the National Lottery or has survived an air crash, he is entitled to give priority to his own thoughts. Even in such a case, as objective an account as possible of his experience and his feelings rather than a long wail of incoherent pain will be of greatest interest to his readers or viewers.

Whether a single source is enough for a story, especially a controversial story that is likely to be challenged, is a debatable question. Can a single source be more than a corner-cutting trick?

Most journalists would agree that it is better to consult more than one source if more than one is available; but that, on occasion, when a single source is the only one available, the legitimate trick is to use it carefully and shrewdly. In fairness to journalists, it must always be borne in mind that, especially when a journalist is dealing with sensitive and crucial public issues, such a single source may indeed be all that is available, and that if that source is in a position to know what he is talking about, and the need for disclosure of some sort of malpractice is powerful enough, then the journalist is morally entitled to do the best he can with that single source. It might be thought that the fact that the story *is* based on a single source should be made clear to the reader. But, particularly when he is dealing with an unidentified source, it must be emphasized that such a disclosure may lead to the identification of the source.

There may even be cases where any attempt to procure a second source for an allegation of some sort of malpractice may be counter-productive – especially if the second source is the very organization whose members are allegedly responsible for the malpractice. Laymen may think it an unacceptable trick if a journalist does not refer an allegation to the people against whom it has been made. But in practice doing this can often lead to an unsatisfactory outcome.

Either the person or people at whom the accusing finger has been pointed will deny the whole thing and say nothing more; or they will approach other journalists who are more favourably inclined towards them and supply a 'spoiling' story that will put them in a better light than in the rival newspaper or on the rival television or radio station; or they will look for some way to kill the story before it is published by recourse to lawyers and injunctions. Provided the journalist is sure of his sources and his facts, *not* inviting such sabotage of his story may, in this sort of context, be a morally acceptable journalistic trick.

With this proviso, the quality of a piece of journalism can often be measured by the number and spread of its sources. Sources, it cannot be said too often, mean work. There are few if any short cuts. Even those who are far from being fans of Karl Marx will probably agree with his maxim that 'value equals work'. It certainly applies to the collection and questioning of sources, and no amount of journalistic trickery in presentation will long conceal a shortage of work and value from knowledgeable and media-savvy readers, viewers or listeners.

Sources are especially valuable to journalists who are working on running stories. But they can sometimes be more valuable still: when they supply the basis for new and unexpected stories which, for the public, come out of the blue.

25

The Unexpected

How often do you find something quite unexpected in a newspaper? At the present time too rarely. The dominant journalistic trick is to try to provide a multitude of variations on a small number of easily recognizable and therefore permissible themes – broadly, those that have celebrity, sex, disaster or scandal appeal.

By and large, the 'culture' of national newspapers and radio and television channels is to compete on the same big stories. That trick is what gives their executives the satisfaction of feeling part of a great psychodrama, in which they may increase their own reputation, do their rivals down and ingratiate themselves with their money-men bosses, who may or may not know or care much about journalism as such but may be impressed by the latest quote from a David Beckham or a David Cameron, or someone else who may be still in the public eye when this book appears.

Of course, big stories must consume the lion's share of journalistic time. But it is arguable that the journalism of two generations ago was more 'human' in its understanding of the need for light and shade, and for the blending of the big story, which most readers would automatically search for, with idiosyncratic contributions that would take the reader by surprise and make him feel he had been given a free bonus.

A few days before the second world war broke out, when newspapers were full of the depressing speeches of Chamberlain, Hitler, Stalin and Roosevelt, the London *Evening News* ran a short piece on the public clock on the tower of St

George's Hospital at Hyde Park Corner. It had slowed down, or stopped, several times in the past, but it was now running at full speed – backwards.

It might be said that at a time when Britain was expecting the full weight of Hitler's Blitzkrieg, which had already bull-dozed and over-run much of Europe, a story about a hospital clock running backwards should deserve little attention. But it could also be said that at times of national or international anxiety, the small 'human' story has increased attractions for readers. It is a reminder that despite the horrors of great politi-cal events, life goes on in all its variety.

In this particular case, the story had resonances that were especially suited to the timing. 'Making the clock go back-wards' was perhaps what was in the minds of millions of people as they were being swept inexorably into world war. Without being entirely fanciful, the earlier slowings-down and stopping of the clock could be seen as a metaphor for the pub-lic's reluctance to being swept into war.

In other words, the story had things going for it in terms of both the 'go-for-the-big-one' and the 'go-for-the-contrast' schools. The unpredictable and idiosyncratic story that some-how chimes in with the dramatic events everyone is talking about, is gold dust. Gold dust is rare. Usually the best a news-paper can do is simply to find an idiosyncratic and unexpected story of any kind.

Some journalists will regard this area of activity as a side-show. So it may be, but sideshows can be an important part of any circus. They may need to be hunted out. But a reporter who takes the trouble to do so is not wasting a news editor's time. It is all too easy to fall into the – to use the expression made famous by the great film *Casablanca* – 'Round up the usual suspects!' approach.

It works like this. Names make news. A name comes up in the news. Let us say it is the name of a minister who accepts a loan from another politician to buy an expensive house. Round up the usual suspects! Or, to put it another way, get the staff to do all the predictable stories. Ask the political editor to write the main news story. Ask the political correspondent to talk to MPs about whether the minister should resign or hold on. Ask the political reporter to write about cases in the past where loans have given politicians trouble. Ask the property editor/correspondent/reporter to write about property values in the area where the minister has his house. Ask the agony aunt to write about what it must feel like for a wife to face the possibility of having an unemployed, and conceivably homeless, husband, and how she should be dealing with her situation. Send the most junior reporter out into the rainy street to ask a collection of passers-by what they think should be done to the minister. Ask the second most junior reporter to write a 'think piece' on whether ministers cut themselves off from the wavelength of the general public when they live in expensive houses.

And so on, and so on. Each of these journalistic tricks would be valid. But also predictable. It would be more imaginative if, as well, someone (perhaps a bright young reporter) suggested interviewing a family in Newcastle facing eviction from their council house, and asking them what they thought about their situation by comparison with that of the compromised minister.

It would be even more imaginative if someone (perhaps that same bright young reporter) were to find a story that had nothing to do with government ministers or houses, but was simply light relief or a complete antithesis to the main news story. Are there foxes in Westminster Abbey, as suggested by the messes found in there? Why has the Darlington professional conjuror disappeared? Do traces of bloodstained cloth at Stonehenge indicate black magic rituals? Is the new drug being developed by an international drugs company a cure for baldness?

A word of caution in reading 'unpredictable' news stories. Do not be too surprised if the 'centuries old traditional cheddar-cheese-rolling down Buttercombe-on-Sea's main street', which the local council cruelly wants to end, is a 'tradition' that was thought up by some enterprising freelance journalist in a silly season a mere thirty years ago.

In the main, the more worthwhile unpredictable stories are those which are more than merely idiosyncratic. I remember the sense almost of physical shock I experienced when, without prior knowledge, I read in *The Guardian* a piece by the paper's then Soviet bloc specialist Victor Zorza about his daughter's experience of life in a cancer hospice, and his feelings about that and about her death. Restrained, and without the 'I'm totally devastated!' cliché, it was an unpredictable piece that stayed in the memory for infinitely longer than stories about the main news events of the day. Investigations of important subjects that may not already be in the news, but that have social value and make human impact because they are new rather than predictable, also justify their space.

Journalism is not written primarily as history, but it is the unpredictable, rather than the predictable saturation coverage of news events, that may have the greater shelf life in public memory. By ignoring the unpredictable as 'irrelevant', newspapers and other news vendors may be weakening their contemporary appeal as well as their value to the historian.

But I am certainly not thinking mainly of the cosy animal stories that used to be told habitually to round off some television news programmes. Monkeys that hold tea-parties or smoke cigars are in their own way as predictable as the variations on the theme of the minister who is both in the news and up the creek.

Stories about over-exposed personalities, whether in Parliament or the zoo, or in venues in between like theatres or football fields, can amount to a trick that can paradoxically make our political, intellectual, artistic and moral leaders even more vulnerable than they may be already.

26

In Yer Face, Or Hello, Goodbye

A widespread and possibly unconscious journalistic trick, when reporting on the doings of celebrities, is to push them so far into the public's face that the public soon resents their constant presence in its life and comes to loathe them (and possibly the journalist involved, too).

This trick could, in practice if not by intention, be part of an 'ill-will machine'; but it could also be accidental: the result of excessive zeal in pursuing known names. If it is part of an ill-will machine, it might be a conscious or unconscious trick to discredit and kill off celebrities the journalist has created – or thinks he has created – five minutes ago, to make room for even newer names. What is certain is that creating celebrities and then writing about the minutiae of their lives until both journalists and the public tire of them is far easier work than finding out what is really happening in politics, business, the arts and sport.

An unusual example in recent years of the forcing on the public of more knowledge about a celebrity than it can cope with was the case of the novelist and essayist Martin Amis's false teeth. It was, and remains, a clear demonstration of how over-exposure can undermine the enthusiastic and sympathetic welcome that celebrities can expect to receive from the public – at least at first.

Gossip columns were bursting with stories about how Amis, who had acquired an American agent and was in a relationship with an American woman, was spending $30,000 on private dental work, at a time when the inadequacies of the National Health Service in treating less privileged members of the public were beginning to receive a lot of publicity.

To many readers, $30,000 on dental work (however necessary it may have been in fact: it included replacement of part of his jawbone) must have seemed like conspicuous over-consumption. Amis had previously received a lot of personal publicity, portraying him as diminutive but street-wise Mart, leader of the literary pack and award winner de luxe. This characterization might have been designed for the delectation of travelling salesmen, frequenters of the Groucho Club and football hooligans – and to bring about the alienation of people who were likely to read his books, or any books, without moving their lips.

After coming across more than several references to Amis's dental work, one was tempted to react in this way: 'I am sick to death of this over-hyped, over-rated man and his bloody $30,000 false teeth! I do not want his false teeth to be with me at breakfast, lunch and the ten o'clock news before I turn in!

I cannot *stand* a man whose false teeth are more famous than he is! I wish he would speedily go to America, or somewhere even further away, and stay there.' Which is more or less what he actually did at around that time.

If one was to be fair, however, one would have had to back away from such hostile reactions and coldly ask oneself a few pointed questions, the last of which would be: 'What is *really* happening here?'

The first would be: 'Have I ever met this man and been insulted by him, or have I any other sort of personal grievance against him?' The answer would almost certainly be no.

The second question would be: 'Do I consider his actual work to be rubbish?' The answer would possibly be: 'On the contrary, I read his early novel, *The Rachel Papers*, with interest, and found it sympathetically conceived and cleverly constructed; and I have read most of his novels since. *Success* and *Money* are perceptive studies of how crude drives can distort lives; and *Other People* must be one of the most evocative accounts of what it must feel like to be insane since Kafka's *Amerika*. He may be over-hyped, but he has talent.'

The third would be: 'Do I resent success as such?' To which the answer would be: 'No. Did I ever resent Graham Greene? No, I admired him. Did I ever resent Mart's father, Kingsley Amis? No. I grabbed his novels as they came out.'

The fourth question would be: 'Do I resent successful people as such?' The answer: 'This is a more difficult one. I am aware that all success entails bullshit, and I do not like bullshitters as a species, especially when they are close at hand, although I can certainly stand them at a distance. In any case I do not believe that $30,000 worth of false teeth would be the *sort* of bullshit any man in his right mind would deliberately conjure up to promote himself.'

Quite. One's splurge of hostility against the industrious Amis and his expensive teeth was caused primarily, not by anything Amis had done or was, but by resentment at having his false teeth – if an appropriate metaphor may be used – constantly crammed down one's throat. In other words, it was less what Amis had done that caused the hostility than what the journalists reporting on the important matter of his teeth had done.

The fact is that the news media are a far more powerful, inescapable presence today than they ever were in the past. It is safe to assert that journalists would be able to pick on almost any individual, including a Mother Teresa figure, and, by reporting on every conceivable detail of her or his life, make the public detest them and sigh for their early disappearance.

Consider another example. 'Posh Spice' Victoria Beckham and her husband, the footballer David Beckham (if they have not, by the time this book is published, so far receded from public view that their names need lengthier explanation) have been made to suffer in this way. Even if the trick has in some ways been of advantage to them, even if in some ways they may have enjoyed the ride, they have in a sense been the victims of a journalistic trick.

Victoria was a modestly talented member of a – for a time – popular singing group, the *Spice Girls*, and her life was therefore of some interest. David Beckham at the time of writing is still a talented footballer whose views on football might have been of interest, and whose life has also been of some interest as a result. But appearing in newspapers each and every day, as they have done, and quite often in glossy fan magazines who pay money for the right to write emollient banalities about you, will have another effect. It may have led not only to increased adulation but also eventually to a public sensation of over-feeding, if not severe indigestion, and to resentful thoughts.

Royalty opened the door to a measure of personal publicity some years ago, thinking that it would make the monarchy more widely popular. But it has now arguably suffered badly through the trick of over-exposure, to the point where many intelligent people, even though they may not be republicans, may well be thoroughly sick of the tide of triviality about constantly reported-on royal individuals. Did Prince William hunt/drink/smoke/disappear with a girlfriend, or didn't he? Whether or not he did, the constant reiteration of the same questions inevitably becomes boring and insinuates in the public mind, falsely or otherwise, the idea that it is Prince William himself who is boring rather than the blanket coverage.

Readers, viewers and listeners do not want *any* guests *permanently* in their living rooms, and resent those who overstay their welcome through persistent journalistic tricks. If it was only 'celebrities' who suffered it might not be so serious. But at the present time, real celebrities, who must be reckoned part of our national treasure, suffer as well.

For commercial reasons, such tricks of over-exposure may 'have' to be performed. But the results do not 'have' to be read or watched until dislike of the people on view flares up. The mainly downward volatility of tabloid circulations may suggest that the reading public is getting the message. If so, that mysterious if often invoked entity, 'the public', might not deserve to be blamed, as they tend to be now, for many other journalistic tricks.

27

The Encroaching 'Public'

All politicians should be prepared to disclose the size and colour of the underwear they are wearing. The public has a right to know.

Or at least that is more or less what some journalists will tell you. Sometimes their desire for 'transparency' in our leaders is justified, and indeed vital for the health of society. At the same time, it should be borne in mind that journalists have a vested interest in revelations, morally and legally justified or not. They fill newspapers, magazines and the air waves. It is their lifeblood.

The trick of journalists here is to blur the line between necessary and unnecessary information about people with power over us, people who entertain us, or people we have merely heard of in some context or other. There remains a difference between stories that are in the public interest (e.g. infamy in high places) and stories that might interest the public (e.g. the colour of a politician's or a pop star's underwear).

When the 2001 outbreak of foot and mouth was winding down, farmers started to apply to the government for legal compensation for their cattle and sheep that had had to be destroyed in line with the government's policy of the extermination of infected herds. This led to two significant developments. On the one hand, some politicians began to claim that such payments were excessive and that in future the public would expect a policy of vaccination instead of culling so that such claims could be avoided. On the other hand, in the teeth of rumours that some farmers had become millionaires at public expense, some newspapers began to support the public demand for full disclosure of payments to individual farmers.

Such a case is quoted, not out of sympathy for farmers or politicians or journalists, but because it is an ideal illustration of how complicated the rights and wrongs of 'public' demands for full disclosure can be.

No doubt a journalist would be pleased with full disclosure in this case, as in most others: it would fill space and promote the controversy on which journalism thrives. The politicians would have a more ambivalent position: farmers in their constituency would almost certainly be against full disclosure; but voters in general might well be for it. Farmers themselves might well like to know what their principal competitor was being paid, but would be reluctant to divulge their own payments.

In the face of these three different perspectives on disclosure, what is truly right – as distinct from most powerfully defended? Assertions about what 'the public' demanded on the matter of disclosure would tend to be indistinct, especially as the media are naturally more reluctant to commission opinion polls on their own affairs than on other people's.

Journalists have the least to lose and the most to gain professionally by disclosure, and their understandable trick is to obscure this fact by thunderous calls in defence of the public interest. Large corporations owning newspapers, magazines and television stations, all calling for disclosure on almost everything under the sun, might well be more sensitive if their own tax arrangements were mentioned. In this light, calls for the disclosure of the details of other people's affairs, when the reason is not immediately obvious, should be taken with a pinch of salt.

One of the farmers who received large foot and mouth compensation payments from the government, which made him a millionaire, later blamed the government for inflated pay-outs. He claimed that in publishing a list of standard prices the Department for Environment, Food and Rural Affairs had artificially pushed up the values of claims. The result, he stated, was that he, and those farmers who had been paid earlier, had received less than those being paid at the time he spoke. He did not reveal precisely how much he had been paid, but defended himself by saying that when he tried to replace the 460 breeding cows that had been killed, he had been able to buy only 330 new ones of the same quality.

The argument most paraded by journalists, that farmers had been 'made millionaires' by government payments – the argument used to defend the call for full disclosure – was in this case suspect. Obviously if a farmer had 100 cows and was paid £1,000 a cow, he would be paid £100,000; whereas if he had ten times that number of cows, he would be paid £1,000,000 and, such are the miracles of arithmetic, if he had 100 times that number, he would be paid £10,000,000.

The oblique suggestion that the money paid was his own pocket money, which would make him a millionaire able to swan around in the South of France, as distinct from money that was necessary to repair the damage to his herd and keep a hard-working man in business, was as spurious as the calls for full disclosure of (by implication) ill-gotten gains.

This is only one case where the 'public's' right to know has conjured up a picture of a public constantly encroaching on sensitive information possessed by public and private figures that was at least partly inspired by journalists slanting their stories in a particular way.

All demands from the 'public', as relayed by journalists, should be examined carefully and treated with a degree of caution: some might say cynical caution. Is there really, for instance, any public need for an individual farmer to say how much compensation he has personally received? Surely, all the public need to know is what the figure for the compensation being paid per head of cattle or sheep is, and the total cost of the compensation?

Why should you or I have the right to know how much an

individual farmer has been paid unless there is a solid suggestion that payments have been made dishonestly? Why should your neighbours have the right to know how much you have been paid by the insurance company if your house has been burnt down? Does 'the public' have a right to know what an individual journalist is paid?

It may be argued that government funds that we all contribute to should be accountable to all of us. In some cases they should. But if you carry such an argument to its logical conclusion, the 'public', ably represented by journalists, would be entitled to know how much pension a particular elderly widow collects and how much social security money a particular disabled person receives. Such a 'public', whether invented or supported by journalists, would have encroached too far on individual freedom and legitimate confidentiality. If a journalist you talk to denies this, ask him to disclose his exact salary, and his expenses for the past week, and see how far you get. Why should he make any such disclosure? Quite.

If invoking 'the public' can be a journalistic trick to strengthen a story, invoking *publicity* rather than the public can sometimes produce a story in itself, a journalistic trick that creates two stories from the same set of circumstances, perhaps sometimes to compensate for a shortage of hard facts.

28

Or Is It a Publicity Stunt?

A common trick when a journalist doesn't know whether a story is correct or not is to present it as a mystery. In this way ignorance, garnished with innuendo, can almost be an advantage to the journalist, although it may not serve at all well the intelligent reader who wants facts rather than speculation.

Such a trick would not have been so easy to pull off in previous eras when merely implying that a married actress might be having an affair with an actor might have led to the libel courts without delay. In our present era, when some entertainers have lower standards of marital decorum, and will do practically anything for publicity, however dire, resort to the courts is less likely. Inside a rather louche sub-world, recourse to the law is very unlikely indeed unless a journalist suggests that a man or woman is no good in bed, in which case wholesale legal war is almost certain. A suggestion of high-living immorality may be seen as flattering, but the suggestion of someone being an incompetent lover is unacceptable in an age that is mechanistically-minded about sex and tends to think you can mark 'performance' from one to ten.

In practice, it may have become easier to write about the private lives of celebrities without having exact information that would stand up in a court of law. If an actor is seen having dinner at the Ivy restaurant with a voluptuous blonde, and the journalist doesn't know who she is, the sight of them together in public may nevertheless be enough for a 'Star with Mystery Blonde' story. If the journalist does know who she is – say, an actress and singer in musicals – this may be sufficient for the journalist to ask in print whether they are contemplating marriage, or something else. Though we are often told that this age is so much more 'sophisticated' than previous ones (an absurd self-delusion), it seems to be widely assumed that if two people of the opposite sex are seen having lunch or dinner together in a public restaurant, sexual intercourse or marriage or both will be the inevitable outcome.

It may well be that the more absurd the story, the less those written about will be likely to protest. The two parties are unlikely to protest, for instance, if the actor is homosexual and the woman lesbian, and if both parties wish to keep these facts about themselves quiet for the good of their careers. They are also less likely to protest if the man is impotent following a prostate operation, or if one of the parties involved wishes the story were true and the other party does not wish to seem to be publicly and brutally repudiating any suggestion of an involvement.

The relaxation of moral codes has made it possible for journalists to 'report' more easily on the (possible) doings of the famous. This can be a dangerous process for the journalist, however, if the matters written about do come to feature in a court of law, because he may not have bothered to consider the possibility of legal action and prepared his case. But in nine cases out of ten, reports of personal behaviour, however absurd, are ignored, unless the person described in print possesses a cast-iron refutation of the journalist's implications, and has a great need for money and no ready means of obtaining it except through damages for defamation.

A comparatively recent development has made it even easier for journalists who do not know the full facts to write a story, nonetheless. The public is now sophisticated enough in the ways of the publicity scene to know that many stories about stars and celebrities are fed to journalists by publicity agents. This has opened the way for a new type of journalistic trick that was practically unheard of two generations ago. It is the story that exists only by virtue of asking: 'Is This All A Publicity Stunt?'

That is what happened when the popular broadcaster and multi-millionaire Chris Evans was seen out and about with the teenage actress Billie Piper. There was a great deal of solid reporting of his taking the milk-bottles in, or putting them out, at his home; of him wheeling home supermarket trolleys containing large quantities of bottles of beer; and so on. But, amidst it all, the question was posed: was his relationship with the teenager a publicity stunt?

In this case, if it *was*, he married it. But the column inches devoted to the whole episode were increased by the fact that newspapers and magazines could discuss not only whether the romance was off or on, but also whether the whole thing was a stunt. The broadcaster and the actress were perhaps happy to be in the public eye. The journalists were certainly happy. The only people who were conceivably not happy were readers who (1) were seriously interested in either Evans or Billie, and wanted to know the full facts, or (2) readers who were not very interested in Evans or Billie but might have been induced to read two factual paragraphs encapsulating the whole personal situation.

Of course journalists cannot be expected to know the true facts unless someone tells them what they are, which in this area they may or may not be likely to do. In such circumstances, may journalists be forgiven for going ahead on the basis of the best facts they have at their disposal, since their competitors will be doing the same thing? The fact that what they are writing about may in any case turn out to be a publicity stunt gives them the additional licence to churn out whatever facts they do have, *plus* speculation (sometimes amounting to a virtual denial of the rest of the story) about whether it is all a publicity stunt.

In August 2001, the actress Nicole Kidman, famous in Britain for her roles in *The Blue Room* and *The Graduate*, and her separated husband Tom Cruise, who had resolutely denied a long-term homosexual affair recently, were due to appear at the Hollywood premiere of her film *The Others*, which Cruise had co-produced. There was press speculation about who would go with him to the premiere: Kidman, or Penelope Cruz, a twenty-seven-year-old actress he had allegedly fallen in love with when making *Vanilla Sky* with her.

There was much waffle in the glossy magazines about how, for this film, Cruise and Cruz had to be seen to be passionately in love. So were they in fact behaving in accordance with Laurence Olivier's famous dictum, 'It's called *acting*, dear boy'? Cruz herself was quoted as saying, 'We are friends.' She denied she had the habit of trying to split up her leading men, among them Matt Damon and Nicholas Cage, from their lovers, saying that she had had to deal with this sort of story since she was sixteen. She also said she was used to finding pieces in magazines saying she was going to marry a man she didn't even know.

One story made the point that all the parties involved were actors and therefore professional fakers of emotion. And it was also argued that it was 'unfair' for cynics to suggest that the Cruise-Cruz romance was an elaborate stunt cooked up by the two stars' publicity machines. This had the effect of reporting it as a possibility, so that, if in future the story was revealed as twaddle, the journalists could turn round and say, 'Well, we did warn you!' Many column inches were filled with question marks rather than facts.

In fact what happened on the night of the awards was that

Tom Cruise and Nicole Kidman behaved like sane human beings. Kidman arrived first, wearing a black dress, her hair in a ponytail, and a silver necklace. She had a woman friend on either side, Naomi Watts and Rebecca Rigg, and spent some minutes signing autographs outside the Directors Guild of America's screening theatre before walking inside to give interviews.

Tom Cruise arrived twenty minutes later, alone. Asked how he dealt with questions about his divorce and his personal life generally, Cruise replied: 'Tell them to mind their own business.' Few people questioned by journalists seem able to speak like that, presumably because they do not want to antagonize *any* journalist. During the ceremony, contrary to subliminal media messages that they were possibly about to have a ten-round boxing match, or launch missiles at one another, Cruise and Kidman merely avoided one another. End of a story that never was? Not a bit of it. There followed *more* speculation, this time about the twenty-seven-year-old actress Penelope Cruz, with whom Cruise had been linked by, as one newspaper put it, 'Hollywood publicity machines'.

How far journalists may sensibly go in the course of the trick of writing speculation, and then attempting to insure themselves against criticism by asking whether it is all a publicity stunt, is itself speculation. The present trend suggests that they may go a great deal further unless public-relations people stop giving journalists the opportunity of having two stories in one. First, a titbit about the lives of stars that can be published without much effort. Then, when the people concerned in the story deny it, a second story asking whether it was all a publicity stunt. And perhaps there can even be a third story, this time asking why the people concerned *needed* that sort of publicity stunt in the first place.

Essential information, entertainment, or money for threadbare old rope? Whatever this trick amounts to, at least it can be conducted without journalistic trickery towards the people concerned when journalists and subjects are face to face.

29

Closing the Notebook

This case is fictitious but it illustrates a journalistic trick. The government minister has produced a range of soothing platitudes about Britain's future in Europe for the benefit of his journalist interviewer. He points out that a huge proportion of British trade is with European countries, that there are an increasing number of defence problems which concern Europe as a whole and that he is keeping an open mind on the possibility of joining the European Monetary Union.

Blah, blah, blah, blah, thinks the journalist, and shortly afterwards closes his notebook, or switches off his recorder. The politician gives a sigh of relief and says with a laugh that Britain will enter the European Monetary Union and abandon the pound over his dead body, that the whole thing is a 'trick by the Krauts' to dominate Europe as Hitler was not able to do by military methods, and that, to compete with the 'wily Japs' and the 'disciplined Chinks', British workers would have to be paid much, much less, and enjoy fewer expensive welfare benefits than people were at the moment enjoying in most hidebound European countries, if they were not to 'go down the pan' in the face of Far East competition.

These remarks, subsequently used by the journalist to introduce his story, threaten melt-down in the Cabinet and an international crisis. They make the journalist's name a highly marketable commodity, even if he is also regarded as a cheat by politicians. They create a suspicion of Britain in the minds not only of the 'Krauts' and 'Japs' but of all countries who do business with Britain.

It is not so far-fetched. Such things, if in a more minor key, have actually happened. When a journalist closes his notebook or switches off his recorder, it may or may not signify that the interview is now over, and that all that is said from now on is completely off the record. Closing the notebook or switching off the recorder might not have been a possible trick in more 'gentlemanly' times, but it may now occasionally be a trick with the purpose of inciting greater frankness. Unless he specifically asks, 'Are we now off the record?' and the journalist answers, 'Yes,' the minister has no clear right to complain if his unwise remarks are quoted.

It may be a dangerous state of affairs for politicians. But why should the public care?

One of the reasons they should is that the process may make matters of public concern more fogged rather than clearer. This may happen in a number of different ways. Suppose that the journalist questioning the minister is known to be against further European integration and is suspicious of foreigners. The minister gives the open notebook or the running recorder his public stance on Europe but, when he believes he is no longer being reported, *butters up* the journalist by throwing in a few comments that will chime in with his prejudices. He may say to himself: 'Where's the harm? I want to keep on the right side of him, and he won't report the remarks, even though he will appreciate them, because he has signalled that the interview is over.'

In these circumstances, what the public may be getting is not clarification of the politician's real attitudes but only evidence of his showing off or of his trying to appeal to the journalist's prejudices or sense of humour.

If the journalist is a glamorous blonde of either sex, the temptation to show off may be difficult to resist, especially for people as vain as politicians, and especially after the third brandy following lunch. Many politicians have regretted showing off to journalists even without benefit of brandy. But it is arguable that the things that have happened as a result have brought little discernible benefit to the public. In Clement Attlee's post-war Labour government, the Chancellor of the Exchequer was Hugh Dalton, the tall, high-church organ-voiced liker of pretty faces. Meeting a young evening newspaper journalist in the lobby immediately before going into the Chamber of the House of Commons to present his budget, Dalton told him about one of its more important provisions. The journalist got the information into his newspaper before Dalton had announced it in the House of Commons, and Dalton had to resign: financial manipulators could have used it at the expense of those who did not yet know the news.

But all this incident told the general public was that a vain man, not taking into consideration the timing of newspaper deadlines, had found it difficult to keep his mouth shut and resist playing the oracle to an apparently impressionable young journalist. He had not thought the journalist would be able to make the information public before he did so himself in the House of Commons.

Where the reported remarks are less factual and more a question of tone – as with the references to 'Krauts' and the 'Japs' in the earlier scenario – the danger that the act of showing off may be deceptive is greater. Few politicians would lay themselves as open as Hugh Dalton on matters of fact. But all stories in which public figures come out with socially unacceptable sentiments should also be taken with at least a small pinch of salt.

Has the journalist really tricked him into revealing a truth? Or has he merely tricked him into shooting his mouth off as the result of an inflamed vanity, or liver, or of piles? Was the interview a significant battle, or a phoney war?

Such questions may well be subtle ones and have no easy answers. When journalists publicly claim that they are going to 'declare war' on celebrities because of their supposedly ruthless attempts to obtain publicity for themselves, the 'war' may well be a very phoney one indeed: a trick to take the moral high ground without being prepared to earn it.

30

Phoney War

The year after the declaration of war on Germany in 1939 was called the Phoney War because nothing much in the way of hostilities happened during that period. In the summer of 2001, a national daily newspaper ran an article featuring a picture of a dustbin containing some faces well known on the celebrity circuit, including that of the six-foot-two Lady Victoria Hervey, under the heading, 'We declare war on publicity-mad celebrities.'

It was inevitably an even more phoney war than the first year of the second world war. The press declaring war on the sort of people they are glad to use as the basis of stories? It was as if the British had masochistically shipped all their armaments into German-occupied France for the use of Hitler, announcing that that would teach him a lesson.

When any sector of the media suddenly implies it has a down on celebrities, it may be fibbing, with its tongue in its cheek and its fingers crossed. That is the nature of the trick. What 'imitation celebrities' – people at whom cameras are pointed, as distinct from people who have genuinely achieved something – want more than anything else is publicity. They would *prefer* reports of their sainthood, sexual prowess and personal beauty; but anything is better than nothing. They would prefer to be 'made war on' than ignored.

There is only one weapon that is likely to be effective against such 'celebrities', and that is to ignore them. And journalists working for those sectors of the media that create and maintain such paper-thin 'celebrities' cannot afford to do it. They are frightened that if they fail to supply their readers with their daily fill of footballers, models, and 'actresses', their rivals will nip in and do it – and they will lose readers.

The result is that, while as firmly attached to the phoney celebrity circuit as any other part of the media, or even more so, they may periodically feel obliged to stage the trick of pretending to repudiate their insubstantial pets, even to the extent of 'declaring war' on them. In this way they may hope, too, to keep the door open to intelligent or at least not completely moronic readers, while continuing to titillate those who boast a forehead about half an inch high and three inches wide.

It can be a tortuous trick, if for both parties it is a useful one. But it *is* a trick, and not the most convincing one that the more populist quarters of the media can think up. It may be an understandable approach. Human patience with moderately talented exhibitionists may be strong in sections of the public. However, to those who may have to spend the long hours of their working lives penning banalities about them, it may be a sore trial. But war? More often than not, it would be a phoney war.

No one with intelligence would suppose otherwise, or would greatly care about such wars. But do people with intelligence now count for as much as they did? Or are they being made to feel that their intelligence is something for which they should apologize, as they are herded out of centres of activity and into the sidelines?

31

Dumbing Down

Intelligence has become a quality that is seldom talked about. It is one of those forbidden 'elitist' attributes. A visitor from Mars might conclude that intelligence is now perceived on Earth as being almost completely irrelevant to the 'real life' that journalists write about. Almost any other human quality, however trivial, is given more attention, prominence and respect in the broadsheets as well as the tabloids.

Intelligence is not cunning self-interest, and it is not the same thing as intellectuality. It is the quality that enables us to tell what is *actually* happening in any given situation, whatever other people are saying about it, and to steer ourselves accordingly. The reader, listener or viewer is, however, frequently encouraged to desire nothing but personal beauty, money and 'style', the latter being notoriously a preoccupation of those who haven't got any. Intelligence is largely ignored, especially if it is possessed by people who are not photogenic and do not want to prance about at the Groucho Club, or at PR parties, in absurd (but expensive) clothes, wearing other human beings on their arms as trophies or badges.

The effect of this is socially baleful. Those who command attention can be shallow nullities with beauty and money and not much else, while intelligent people are ignored. This is a disaster for society because both public and private affairs demand intelligence for their effective management, the lack of it tending to lead to a messy shambles. And we are now seeing plenty of *those*.

A cynic and doom-monger might suspect that we were being tricked by journalists (and, of course, others: journalists tend merely to follow the trends, whether nice or nasty) into putting our affairs into the hands of those who are the least likely to be able to manage them competently, that is to say, those with minimum intelligence.

We have pictorial 'artists' who are picturesque buffoons without discernible talent. We have art collectors and curators who are less picturesque but have plenty of public or private money at their disposal to orchestrate their minimal judgment of anything except which passing fashions and fads are likely to enhance their careers. We have national politicians who might win a prize for hair-styling or middle management in a small business, but would be over-stretched by anything requiring more than stereotyped careerism. We have businessmen with faces blinkered to anything except the main chance. We have churchmen who playfully pull their cassocks up over their heads on hot days – I have actually seen one do it at a christening – to show that they are not stuck up at all, and others who vacuously parrot the touchy-feely slogans of the moment as a substitute for trying to get people to see that money cannot create human perfection, nor be a satisfactory religion.

The trick of journalists is to keep us reading about, watching or listening to such people. They do that by giving them plenty of space and attention. Admittedly they don't necessarily censor *criticism* of the buffoons – criticism whips up interest – but they never make, imply or act on a judgment of this kind: 'This is piffle and, if reported on at all, it should be reported on as briefly as piffle.'

The whole trick, on the part of the dumbing-down politicians, artists, actors and churchmen, as well as the journalists who write about them, is to propagate the subliminal message: 'Because these people are written about, they must be important. Because they are written about at greater length than some boring inventor, surgeon or nurse, they must be more important than them. Because brain-dead shallowness gets more attention, it must be more "real" and "relevant" than intelligence, assuming that we can remember what intelligence is.'

The encouragement, even if it is encouragement by default, of such an attitude is one of contemporary journalism's least attractive tricks. The defence is often to say in effect: 'Journalism only follows public taste. Who are we to tell the public that they are stupid?'

In an epoch of media saturation, this argument has become disingenuous. Journalism has become a creator as well as a reflector of public taste. Where else does the public get its role models from? Politicians? Hardly. The public scarcely knows them except through the filter of the media, and public contempt for politicians now runs deeper than it has ever done in living memory. Actors? Certainly to some extent they are role models, especially in so far as they are reported on by writing and photo-journalists. Vicars and bishops? Hardly: the churches have never been emptier.

By fashioning their trade for the benefit of the not very intelligent majority rather than for the intelligent minority who might encourage the rest to follow suit, journalists in all parts of the media – not merely the tabloid newspapers – play their part in the dumbing-down process, which intelligent people of all levels of income rail against with increasing despair.

Is it beyond the capacity of journalists and those who employ them to pull a different trick? To begin reporting on intelligence as if it were important, vital, even 'cool' – to use a vapid word which as praise, unlike 'clever' or 'intelligent', is fashionably devoid of any intellectual content or inflection?

If intelligent people were taken more seriously by journalists, and therefore by their public, than unintelligent, if often picturesque, buffoons now are, our society might be richer not only in a monetary sense but also in terms of other human benefits; and intelligent journalists might be spared a degree of the self-disgust that is occasioned by the kind of people their executives choose for them to write about, and the way they have to write about them.

They might also find that the people they are dealing with could be written about interestingly without their having to resort to the trick of 'badgering' which is sometimes used not only to set up a story but to be the *basis* of the story itself.

32

Answer! Answer! Answer! Answer!

Asking a politician persistent questions, or the same one repeatedly, without giving him a chance to respond, and then accusing him of evasion, or at least of giving the impression that he is being evasive, is a journalistic trick that is perpetrated haphazardly, perhaps the result of a combative spirit or else intentionally as a means of discrediting the politician (it is usually a politician), whatever he says or doesn't say.

Either way, it is a trick that does less for the cause of truth than the apparent signs of raging battle might suggest. Its effectiveness in revealing truths may be considerably less than meets the eye. Most politicians are quite skilful – and they are becoming even more skilful out of necessity – at repeatedly dodging the demand for an answer until the questioner looks and sounds rude. (See chapter 1.)

Those repeated demands for an answer can create the sense of a field sport such as fox-hunting, or a ring sport like boxing, but in practice they often substitute sound and fury for revelation. The badgered politician will almost certainly have been evaluated already by the viewer or listener, who will regard him, according to their own political views, in the same way during the interview and at the end of it as they did at the beginning: as an evasive cad or a badgered darling.

The 'Answer! Answer!' (or words to that effect) demand is a trick that is useful not to the public but to the journalist, who may well appear to the unsophisticated to be unafraid of Big Wheels and valiant in his campaign against evasion. It can, however, be attitudinizing rather than questioning, and in some cases might perhaps be better performed in front of a mirror than a microphone or camera.

As a trick to convince the public that something is being achieved, it is valid to the extent that something *is* being achieved: the journalist is looking and sounding good. Because he, rather than the person he is interviewing, is doing most of the talking, his vanity – which might be injured by the sight and sound of him clearly failing to reveal anything of substance – is appeased.

So reiterated demands for answers can be a psychological trick rather than a strictly investigatory one, a trick of acting rather than journalism. To a degree cameras have willy-nilly converted television reporters into performers. But performances that enhance the reporter's ego rather than the public's stock of concrete facts, retreat further and further from the requirements of journalism. They can easily become tricks of verbal and visual self-aggrandisement.

'Answer! Answer!' is what opposition parties ritually shout at government ministers in House of Commons debates. It is the rallying cry of political enemies rather than the probing skill of journalism, and it should be suspected of being a trick when it poses as the latter.

This is not to say that journalists who have the trick of probing deeply are necessarily unfair. Provided that they put themselves mentally in the position of an intelligent member of the public, and ask questions that member of the public would like to ask if he had the chance, and in a way he might ask them, any trickery is probably legitimate and benevolent in intention and result. It is undoubtedly maddening when interviewees are evasive, but bullying in response will almost certainly be self-defeating, as well as being irritating to the viewer or listener (obviously, it is usually the viewer or listener rather than the reader), who is lost in a cross-talk row that makes it impossible to hear what is being said by anybody.

Truths cannot be forcibly prised out of people who are clammed up. The *seductive* question, the one the interviewee somehow wants and needs to answer, is the trick that is most likely to be productive and satisfactory to the intelligent public. Will we be lucky enough to encounter more and more of them, rather than fewer and fewer?

It might be useful, too, if the trick of hyping certain stories by suggesting that their content is apocalyptic, when it is often less than that, was given a well-deserved rest.

33

Gone for Ever?

Eras come to an end with bewildering frequency, at least as reported by journalists. Things will 'never be the same again' about twice a week. Not only are eras ended. They are ended *for ever.*

All of which can be the trick of melodramatic hype. To illustrate the point, one cannot do better than look at how the Conservative Party disappeared for ever at least twice, as the natural party of government in Britain. In the first case, it brought to an end for ever the Conservatives as the establishment party – until the Conservatives got into power again.

The point is not a political one. It is an illustration of the journalistic trick of conjuring up terminal mayhem out of the less dramatic pendulum-swinging character of real life. In 1970, Britain looked back on a decade in which Labour had been in power for longer than the traditionally 'usual' government of the Conservatives. Pundits agonized about what this meant. Surely it meant that the era of Conservative dominance, broken up by brief periods of more radical rule from the Liberals or Labour, had come to an end? Surely it must mean that Labour was now the natural 'establishment' party in Britain?

This was a bewitching thesis, especially as the new is always better news than the old to journalists. Faced with the general election of June 1970, most pundits had no difficulty in deciding that Labour under Harold Wilson was going to win again, and that the Conservatives under Edward Heath were done for as the 'establishment' party. The then Labour Home Secretary, James Callaghan, challenged one journalist – it happened to be me – to provide or suggest any evidence at all that change was in the air. Callaghan assured me that there was none: that Labour would be returned as a demonstration that it was now the *usual* government of Britain.

I happened to have been asked to do a broadcast the day after polling day on what the result of the election meant. On the evening of polling day, I sat on Hampstead Heath near my home writing a script about what Labour as the new establishment party would mean to Britain. As I wrote, I heard the buzz of constant traffic around the Heath. I thought to myself that the Conservatives, certainly the natural car-users, must be out in force, and that it might be as well if I were to write an alternative script about what it meant that Labour had in fact been defeated, and that the Conservatives had scraped back with a chance to be the 'establishment' party once again – as they had usually done in living memory.

It was the latter script I had to use. Against almost all pundit opinion, the Conservatives under Edward Heath were elected, and the emergence of Labour as 'the new establishment party' did not happen. An era was *not* ended, as the tricks of pundits had led the public to expect.

In the 1980s and 1990s, the same thing happened to Labour, but in reverse. Michael Foot, a cultured intellectual, became the leader of the Labour Party (incidentally against the predictions of most pundits, who backed Denis Healey). He wore a donkey jacket at the Remembrance Day service at the Cenotaph in Whitehall, and generally became the symbol of the 'obvious' unelectability of the Labour Party, which had outlived its usefulness, lost its direction, and generally ruled itself out of the running for ever and ever as a ruling party, and so on.

With Mrs Margaret Thatcher in 10 Downing Street for the Conservatives, making herself popular by resisting the invasion of the Falkland Islands by the Argentinian military junta, Labour was regarded by some journalists as ditched for ever. Even when Neil Kinnock was made leader of the party and had set himself the task of making it electable by curbing the power of the hard left, Labour still lost the 1992 general election, in which the Conservatives were returned under John Major. Surely this was proof that Labour was ditched *for ever*?

But in the 1997 general election, in which the Conservatives were so unpopular because of fresh revelations of 'sleaze' almost every day, Labour walked into power and the 'era-gone-and-gone-for-ever' trick was now re-applied to the Conservatives.

There are two possible explanations for the 'gone for ever' trick of seeing Armageddon in every pendulum swing. The first is that journalists tend on the whole to be on the young side, so that for them the changes within a period of, say, ten years seem to them great and irreversible movements in history rather than little blips on the screen of life. The second is that journalists have a vested interest in cranking up events so that they seem more dramatically interesting than they really are, and so have perfected this process as a journalistic trick.

Either explanation is comprehensible. But, one way or the other, the pattern does suggest that irreversible ends of eras, when announced by journalists, should be treated with caution.

So, for that matter, should reliance on sex and sexual innuendo as a trick to pep up stories that may in fact have little to do with sex.

34

Sex

It would be unjust to accuse journalists of sole responsibility for making *reading* and *talking* about sex a modern obsession. Advertisers and marketing men are far more responsible. Increasingly, to the point of the absurd, they seek to use sex as a bait to capture their ideal customers: those who are thinking constantly about sex, especially 'perfect sex', and are therefore inevitably dissatisfied and disappointed in that and then almost every other respect – and may be too dim to detect the essentially commercial consumerist trick being played on them.

But journalists do have to take their share of the blame. If dragging sex into everything is essentially a marketing tool aimed at transforming sentient beings into twitchy and grasping 'must-have!' babies, journalists have perfected a similar trick for catching and holding the attention of not very bright readers, listeners and viewers.

It has been developed since the end of the second world war. When British car-makers were trying to sell the first civilian vehicles to come off the production lines since war broke out in 1939, they found that a pretty and prettily dressed model (or mannequin as they were then known), sitting on the car bonnet, gave the photographers an inducement to pay attention to their car rather than their competitors' car. It produced an effect precisely because glamorous and well-dressed models were not to be seen everywhere.

The position today is quite different. With topless models, who would have been regarded as obscene in the 1940s and 1950s, having now become an acceptable norm, advertisers and journalists have become increasingly desperate and decreasingly tasteful in their attempts to capture the attention of coarsened readers and viewers. Whereas once mild sexual titillation would be briefly introduced to an audience, now every conceivable commodity, or subject, is not thought to be 'aggressively sold' unless there is some resort to attempted sexual arousal or innuendo.

Scan the headings in any broadsheet newspaper, never mind the tabloids, and you will see that sex and sexual innuendo are dragged in with predictable frequency and in a mechanistic way that might leave the cynical with the impression that sex is not a real and important constituent of life but a sort of mystical mechanical science that is worshipped from afar by those with no actual experience of it.

'Sex Lives Go Down the Pan' was one of the more permissible headings in a quality newspaper, since it was over the review of a play called *The Shagaround*. 'A Pin-up at the Proms' was the heading of an interview with the 'heart-throb violinist' Joshua Bell, as he prepared to play Bernstein at the Royal Festival Hall. That was going halfway down the slippery slope towards sexual innuendo, presumably in the hope of interesting people who would not otherwise be interested in Bell, Bernstein or indeed anything going on at the Royal Festival Hall.

After these headings had appeared in a newspaper that need not be identified because it was no worse than almost any other, I felt that a complete examination of the headings in one day's issue of an indisputably quality newspaper seemed desirable. In the main section, no such references were found, but in the second, tabloid section of the newspaper, the book-review pages were trailed on the front page with the announcement that 'Beryl Bainbridge Flirts with Dr Johnson', signifying that she had written a novel about that distinguished wit, moralist and dictionary compiler.

Inside the second section, there was an article on the latest fad in Los Angeles, the aerobics strip-tease class, headed 'Flex, Pump and Grind', with a photograph spread over seven columns showing members of such a class, breasts and chest-hair, though not necessarily on the same person, being very much to the fore. In this case, it was the subject itself which was obtrusive: since it had been decided to feature this material, it could hardly be introduced in anything but a sexual fashion.

Further on, however, there was an article which did not need to be introduced by any sexual reference. It was on prepayment cards for under-eighteens. It was headed, 'Teens Learn Art of Safe Spending' – an obvious reference to that well-ventilated subject of sexual concern, safe sex.

There was nothing unusual or over-the-top by contemporary standards in these appeals to sexual interest. The extent of the coverage would have been about the same in any broadsheet newspaper, while in newspapers tailored for the not quite so cerebral elements in society, sexual references might be blatantly explicit rather than gentle hints.

Using sex as a selling implement, whatever the real subject matter, is a trick that has unfortunate effects. It encourages the reader, listener or viewer to think that he is missing out if he is not thinking about sex all the time: an illusion that is very bad for the conduct of day-to-day business, which will mostly have no bearing on sex at all. It encourages a consequent sense of personal inadequacy in those who believe that there is a crowd 'out there' who are having a better time sexually than they are, and may be more sexually attractive/potent. They may come to believe, poor things, that they must in some way be deficient because they are *not* thinking about sex as they go to work on a wet Monday morning. Isn't it more likely that a genuinely highly-sexed person would find the thought of sex a confounded nuisance on the way to work when it was not possible to do anything about it?

The second unfortunate effect is that the introduction of sex into everything means that there is a danger that it may end up being thought of by the disillusioned as being of no importance to *anything*: an exploded salesman's ploy and nothing else. It may be good for the short-term interests of the salesman and the marketing man – and the lazy journalist who depends on an easy trick – but it may be bad for something of greater importance: the survival of a sentient human species.

In real life, a person who talks about sex all the time is a bore, and possibly a self-deceiving bore: someone who is desperately trying to work something worthy of attention into a life he secretly considers to be dull, as he misses out on the grand passions other people are enjoying. Those elements of the media who do the same thing, and those journalists who work for them, may be perpetuating a trick that could be heading for its sell-by date. But in the meantime it can be pathetically childish rather than saucy, and perhaps does us little good in the eyes of those who would be glad to dismiss us as a clapped-out force.

If reliance on sexual images and sexual innuendo in print journalism may be an attempt to compete with the now dominant medium of television, it may also be one more reason why some print journalists have a hostile and denigratory attitude to television. It may well be the case that the amount of drivel on television is increasing year by year. But hostility to television from those in print journalism can be worth examination.

35

Anti-TV Prejudice

Wouldn't you expect newspaper journalists to be potentially resentful of television and those who appear on it?

Most tabloid journalists, and not a few who work for broadsheets, now seem to spend too much of their professional lives trawling for tittle-tattle about people whose importance to the world is clearest to populists. The writing was on the wall when, some years ago, the *editor* of a respected national newspaper queued up in Los Angeles to interview the greatly hyped popular singer Madonna, rather than sending the newest recruit in his reporters' room. It was a gesture in deference to the mores of entertainment and populism that was not widely seen as being out of step with the mores of quality print journalism.

The awareness of those who remain in the print medium that it is no longer dominant; their awareness of how their own career chances have shrunk; and their consequent pique – they are all perfectly understandable. It may also be consoling as well as entertaining when the idiosyncrasies of other people, especially if they are rich and famous, are exposable. But doubt is justified when journalists claim that some of these exposures matter in any significant sense.

Let us say that Heather Hither is a star of the fictitious popular TV soap-opera *West Street*. Ms Hither has had no experience of acting via acting school, little theatres or bit parts in films. She first made her mark when she won a beauty contest in which one of the judges was a television producer who needed the publicity as much as she did, his career being then, as it continued to be, in free-fall. She and he were an 'item' until she met the producer of *West Street*. She subsequently announced to the tabloids that she had at last found a man who made her 'feel like a woman', while his wife announced to them that she would always be grateful to her for relieving her of an utter shit. And so on.

Having 'made' her, they – in this case, the journalists rather than the producers – eventually decide it would be equally good fun, for them and their readers, to first taunt and then destroy her. They put her £100 fine for possessing cannabis onto the front page, where her 'romances' have previously featured. During her second year on *West Street*, she is busted twice more for cannabis possession, and is given a heavier fine for driving up the M1 with three times the legal limit of alcohol in her blood, and trying to change her spectacles while driving, which results in a near-crash and leads to a driving ban for twelve months: an event which somehow attracts fewer headlines and column inches than her sexual mishaps.

All these events have been zealously reported as if she were Queen Elizabeth I instead of an actress who had as yet received very few comments on her *acting*, and those mostly lukewarm or critical.

Then her car, driven by her brother, is flagged down by the police on the M4 as she is in the back enjoying herself with yet another producer, while her brother in front is being given compensatory attention by the producer's sister, beside him.

'We could hardly believe it,' said Sergeant Fred Duck, before going on to explain in detail what it was that he and his equally hard-working colleagues could hardly believe, those details appearing prominently in the tabloids.

It is necessary to ask the question: what exactly have we here? A mediocre actress and tacky woman has appeared in a soap-opera playing a character who could hardly help being more interesting than *she* is. She has not murdered anyone, she has not betrayed anyone whose sense of loyalty is better than her own, she has not persuaded any minors to share her addiction to cannabis, she has not done the theatre arts much good; but, on the other hand, she has not actually set fire to the Royal Academy of Dramatic Art.

So in what sense does the public have to be protected from her, which is the moral claim newspapers and magazines have for pursuing her? It certainly needs to be protected from drunk driving, the escapade in which the crusading press took the least interest. However, revealing the rest of her behaviour at length does not serve the public interest, but only the prurient interest of rubber-neckers.

It would be naive not to see that, at a time when their

primacy as a news source has been usurped by TV, newspaper journalists have a vested interest in stemming the fall in their circulations by publishing lewd material connected with the hybrid monster of television under the cover of protecting the public interest. It would be equally naive not to see that in perpetuating this trick, especially when television 'personalities' or 'celebrities' play a role, print journalists love doing their work more than mere venality would account for. They are able to be passengers on the far-reaching supertanker of television and those associated with it, while at the same time doing harm to the institution and the individuals involved with it, and all for the highest motives: safeguarding the public interest and morality.

The trick is always to make it seem as if the events are of public concern, when as often as not they are further examples of daft people behaving daftly. The result is material that almost certainly, and sadly, shows less intelligence than the journalists writing it possess.

It may also be an example of the over-simplified or distorted motives attributed to people who are the subjects of stories, which would sometimes be more appropriate in a novelette than in journalism.

36

Woolly Motives

Journalists may contribute conspicuously to public confusion about what human beings and life are actually *like*. This is their trick: they supply dangerously woolly or false (though perhaps picturesque) versions of people's possible motives that may cause muddle in the minds and lives of their readers, listeners and viewers.

A useful illustration of a trick which often occurs would be someone writing that, for women, 'power is a great aphrodisiac'. This would be remarkably shallow or obtuse, allowing a certain sort of grasping woman to rationalize her attitude to men by looking at it through rose-tinted spectacles, so that her motives appear to her to be little different from those of any girl who marries or shacks up with someone for love, or at least because of spontaneous sexual attraction.

A colder observer might come to the conclusion that when women marry or consort with power, it is debatable whether 'aphrodisiac' considerations come into it. A woman takes a business decision to open her legs to a rich and powerful man rather than to a poor, powerless one. A young man lines his pockets by fornicating with an older but wealthier woman. Where do aphrodisiac qualities come into it? Where, for that matter, does sex come into it? A decision has been taken on essentially different grounds: commercial ones. Only woolly thinking, occasionally fostered by journalists who deal in woolly over-worked phrases that distort motives, thoughts and emotions, prevents this from being clear. Thus might a cynic argue.

He might go on to reason that if such woolly writing about alleged aphrodisiac qualities is generally flattering to the people written about, there are further journalistic tricks based on woolly thinking about motives that denigrate the people being discussed.

When 'celebrities', or even genuine celebrities, are questioned, the questioning is often a search for dog's motives (with apologies to dogs) based on an unstated assumption that people do not *ever* act with more disinterested motives. The use of the word 'disinterested' has been corrupted so that it is now used as if it meant the same thing as 'uninterested'.

'Prime Minister, you seem to be regarded by the electorate as disinterested in the public health issue.'

To which any literate Prime Minister would be entitled to reply: 'I certainly hope so. I have absolutely no intention or hope of profiting personally from the public health issue. My aim is to lead a country in which all citizens, rich and poor, can receive adequate medical treatment when and where they need it.'

As we know, disinterested is the opposite of self-interested, not a synonym for uninterested. But there is now so little confidence among some journalists that people can act from disinterested motives which are based on an imaginative desire to change and improve things, whether it is the country, an industry or a tennis club, that the reader, listener or viewer is left with the depressed feeling that no one can be trusted at all.

All this can be derived from thinking that is just as woolly as the thinking of those who insist that basically mankind is, essentially, wonderfully decent and lovely until people are upset by something or other, in reality upset by life, which upsets us all in one way or another, although we do not all resort to fraud or murder.

Logically, the search for dog's motives can only be relevant in so far as there is a possibility that other motives may be operating. Why go out of your way to dig out dog's motives if you, and everyone else following your line of thought, knows that they *must* by definition be there? It would be like strenuously trying to prove that the Pope was religious.

The belief or attitude among journalists – or anyone else for that matter – that every action is a bid for power, influence, money or sex is the mirror image of a woolly-minded willingness to believe that real people are as they appear in their own self-flattering words in glossy fan-magazines. It is the same unrealistic perception, but in reverse gear.

To put it bluntly, the Victorian Prime Minister William Ewart Gladstone may or may not have been sexually attracted by the prostitutes he roamed the London streets to save from their degraded life. But even if he had been sexually attracted, it would prove only that he was a heterosexual man, not that he was a hypocrite. His motives in this respect were to all intents and purposes disinterested. It would be a relief if more contemporary journalists could master the trick of seeing such a point clearly through the fog of hype or denigration in much contemporary thought about possible motives.

But what of the motives of politicians who, having no other source of income, are totally dependent on their Parliamentary salaries and the journalists who write about them – and who either puff or abort their careers? What effect does it have on the politicians and the journalists? Some people argue that the dependence in question is desirably 'democratic'. Why do journalists often go along with this? Is it a trick to keep politicians more under their control and advance their careers?

37

My Beautiful Career

It may be argued that if politicians always tailor their answers to suit their career prospects rather than with a view to bringing about broader public benefits, that problem is created by the politicians themselves rather than by the journalists who question them.

It is certainly not the journalists' fault that most British politicians now indulge in politics as a full-time career, and possess no other professional means of supporting themselves if they fail to be re-elected. They are now in hock not only to a fickle public but also to party leaders who, by promoting them or failing to promote them, are able to regulate how much money they have in their pockets, and to the journalists who write about them and thus influence their careers. The days are long gone when aristocrats, usually Tory ones, would do their duty to their class by tearing themselves away from their country estates, and when industrialists, usually Whig ones, would do their duty to the needs of commerce by tearing themselves away from their factories, in order to help run the country to their advantage. Such men could put up two fingers, as it were, to anyone who tried to manipulate them because if it all went wrong, they could simply take a more direct interest in their estates and factories again.

It is not the journalists' fault that politicians are now schooled, even by some obliging media types, in the art of what to say in public and how to say it, so that they are less likely to drop revealing clangers than before. Or is it, in this case, partly the journalists' fault? It could be argued that journalists must at least share the responsibility since they help to establish the terms of engagement under which politicians have to justify themselves. And those terms of engagement may be seen to encourage glibness and self-protection as opposed to frankness, courage and personal honour.

If a politician is constantly being asked what electoral advantage there is for him in a course of action he proposes, he will gradually be eased into thinking of issues in precisely those careerist terms. Paradoxically, the journalist's trick of digging for careerist motives will not persuade the politician to be more frank and open but it may cause him to become more smoothly aware of his narrow personal interests and motives. The journalist is employing a trick here that can badly back-fire in the medium or long term.

If many politicians now think overridingly in terms of their own careers, so do many journalists. The journalist who makes his name, not with continuously interesting, steady and accurate work, but by some chancer's tactic like using what a politician or other interviewee has said but believed to be off the record, or focusing on a pop singer, actor, actress or footballer and seeing what dirt can be unearthed on them, is more common now than he would have been a generation ago. Such journalists may or may not prosper in the medium to long term. But short-termism is in so many spheres the ruling perspective.

Ambition is a useful tool for actually doing what you think you would like to do. This applies to journalists just as it applies to all sorts of professionals. Ideally, ambition is a source of rough power on a perhaps rough journey that the head and heart nevertheless determine. It is not, or should not be, the dictator of the *nature* of the course of action to be undertaken.

The shrewd reader, listener or viewer may be able to detect when a journalist is on a career flier, and may not regard it as a pretty sight. The thing about beautiful careers is that while they may give narcissistic pleasure to the possessors, they are unlikely to seem beautiful to other people. Even people who cannot articulate why they trust one journalist more than another may be aware that, in general, they do not like people – politicians, journalists, lawyers, architects – who are too full of themselves.

Journalism prepared in the hope of gaining an award, or some other career advantage, is a trick which may be forgiven if the people who are being praised or vilified in the course of it happen to be ones the customer himself would wish to vilify or praise. But fairness and reliability – qualities that have long since been overshadowed, if not eliminated, by enterprising self-hype – are tricks that will have their own rewards in the longer term. As with any activity that is of public importance, the *work*, and how it is done, is more important to the public than the *career*.

How important to the public is this ploy that some journalists now increasingly use in the service of their careers? It is what might be called the trick of the stand-up comic approach to journalism: that is, clamouring for attention by using words and sentences that belong to the music-hall rather than to newspaper or other print journalism.

38

The Stand-Up Approach

Good journalistic style is rooted in lucidity, clarity and an avoidance of clichés and formalized modes of expression. In a sense, it can be argued that the trick of good journalism may produce something less like good literature and more like good, lucid conversation.

But in recent years a distinct proviso has become necessary. One 'conversational' journalistic trick embodies informality to an unwelcome degree by inserting into sentences the written equivalent of nervous coughs, twitches and grunts. They waste time, risk irritating the reader by their substitution for witty construction of sentences, and betray the fact that some forms of journalism have entered, or have tried to enter, the realm of performance art.

The trick consists of inserting words which might well occur in spoken sentences but have no place in written ones, writing being on the whole a tidied-up form of speech, where the words themselves, rather than any vocal inflexion given to them, have to hit home. As here, for instance:

> The violent devotees of football tend to be on the whole ... well, er ... rather thick.

The words 'well, er' seek to establish a conversational atmosphere, with a chortling implication that the words are not being written calculatingly (no doubt an 'elitist' practice) but spoken out loud off the top of the head (no doubt an 'approachable' practice). In fact the tone is quite false and on the printed page the words seem little more than obstructions to the reader. Such words are the legitimate trick of the stand-up comedian, and should be returned to him as soon as possible:

> When Sir Herbert Loamstone assumed the chairmanship of Sundry Enterprises two years ago, one director of the company condemned the record of the resigning chairman who had asked for more time to reach his targets, and said that the situation required a bold hand which would increase the firm's profits by at least twenty per cent inside two years, with no excuses for failure, and no more appeals for more time. Yesterday Sir Herbert appealed to the board for further time to achieve the twenty per cent increase. And the director who two years ago called for no excuses for failure? Hum, oh dear – Sir Herbert Loamstone.

What is the excuse for the 'Hum, oh dear'? It is a clumsy way of giving the slow-witted time to think by saying: 'A singular and ironic circumstance is about to be noted, and I wouldn't want a couch potato like you to miss it, so please remain awake and alert. Here it comes ...' If the reader needs to be alerted to the fact that some irony is on the way, the sentence could have read: 'None other than Sir Herbert Loamstone'. This emphasizes the joke but does not break up the flow of words by introducing into a written sentence what is in effect no more than grunting sounds.

> But do we believe him? Can we believe him? Can we believe any politicians in such circumstances? In answer to the allegations that he had been carrying on an affair with a female researcher

and dining with her on the night in question, the minister denied impropriety and said he was ... ah ... somewhere else at the time.

To indicate a tone of disbelief in a written opinion piece, ingenuity of phrasing is the ideal practice. It should not be necessary for the journalist to resort to the 'um and ah' or 'ho and hum' trick. It merely substitutes a verbal belch for thought. Almost invariably, sentences that are punctuated by ums, ahs and so on are weakly constructed, and do not have a readable logic of their own.

Performance journalism, a variation on the stand-up comic's 'I say, I say! A funny thing happened to me on the way to the studio!' is a trick that began to gain currency in the 1970s, when print journalism had visibly become the progeny of television rather than of literature.

It is, oh, such a waste of time and – ah yes! – an insult to the, um, reader!

Fortunately, there are stories that are not tainted by this form of performance journalism, and which, because of its absence, may illustrate its more habitual presence.

39

A Revelatory Disaster

When terrorists destroyed the two vast towers of the World Trade Center in New York on 11 September 2001, the tragedy illustrated in a negative and ghastly way the need journalists have for their professional tricks. It became apparent because that need was temporarily removed: *anything* about the disaster was of solid interest, without the need of trickery.

The destruction and loss of life proved that when events are real and big enough, and the public is bursting to hear about them, some journalistic tricks not only become unnecessary but are actively unwelcome, like wearing a funny top-hat in an air raid.

The most spectacular and ominous warlike act in the lifetime of most readers, listeners and viewers, the destruction of New York's tallest buildings and the loss of over three thousand lives, temporarily abolished the competition in beguiling triviality that in more normal times disfigures so much of newspapers, magazines and television. One could detect the difference in the public response to the media in general. It was as if their work at that time temporarily made it possible for the world to forgive journalists for their tricks in the past.

For a while, simple, straightforward on-the-spot reporting prevailed. The coverage of a real disaster, instead of a forecast or invented one, reminded readers that journalism at its best is a vital, useful and highly desirable activity despite its shortcomings when peace reigns and there is little of real substance to report, and that, in such circumstances, it can perform the valuable social function it should, ideally, always be able to perform.

The descriptions of the muddle after the first hijacked aircraft hit the north tower, the screaming when the second aircraft hit the south tower, and the suspicion that something cataclysmic was afoot when a third hijacked aircraft hit the Pentagon, the defence headquarters in Washington, were exact and colourful in themselves and had no need of hype or the manipulation of words and sentiments.

It was an example, now more rarely seen, of newspaper and other journalists doing their unique and essential job of reporting hard news rather than producing great blobs of slanted news, or comment and opinion about nothing very much – what is called 'style journalism'. The blobs, however, soon returned.

Emotions among those glued to the print and electronic media were, first, sheer incredulity that anyone should have attacked the bastion of Western commerce at the cost of thousands of lives; then sorrow; then anger at the perpetrators; then, more obliquely, the realization of how dependent democracies are on journalists. For a brief period, the journalist on the street suddenly had seemed more important than the financial manipulators who had taken over their industry and had often seemed to imply they thought the only value in journalism was to make money for managers and shareholders.

The story of the eye-witness who, sitting inside one of the buildings, saw the hijacked aircraft about to hit it, did not require any hype. Neither did the story of the woman who had survived the lesser 1993 terrorist attack on the World Trade Center, and was in her office on the 62nd floor of the north tower at the beginning of the 2001 attack. Through the window she saw an aircraft heading straight towards her. It appeared to be a commercial airliner, but it did not seem as if it had just missed the top of the building by accident, she said. Then it went straight into the building. She had known at that moment that it was not an accident. Ordered to leave by stairs already soaked by water because the fire-extinguishers had been automatically activated, she had not reached the bottom of the building when the other aircraft hit the south tower and it collapsed. When she and others reached the ground, they were blasted with asbestos. This eyewitness was found by a journalist, coated in soot, trying to get transport to take her home. The police had declined to take her because they were far too busy with other things.

Nor did the experiences of the male engineer, who was on the 82nd floor of the 110-storey north tower when the aircraft hit it just above him, require anything but straightforward professional reporting. People around him, he said, had their skin burnt off and were bleeding. There had been no lights. A second blast had blown them out through the street door. He had thought he would die. The reporter left him searching for his wife, who worked on a higher floor.

Celebrities had stories as unvarnished as those of the unknown. Mrs Barbara Olson, wife of the Solicitor-General of the USA, a political commentator and author of a book on Hillary Clinton, wife of the former President, was on one of the hijacked aircraft. She managed to call her husband twice on her mobile telephone. She made the first telephone call directly after take-off and the seizure of the aircraft, but she was cut off in the middle of the conversation. She managed to make another call, describing how all the passengers and crew members had been herded to the back of the aircraft. She described the hijackers' knives but she had seen no other weapons. She asked her husband what instructions she should give the pilot, but as he was held captive along with everyone else, there was nothing the pilot could do. Within minutes, she and everyone else on the plane were dead in a fireball.

The reporting of these events and their human price was classic journalism, replete with facts that needed no sensationalizing, editorializing or souping up to make them more accessible to readers.

It was predictable that the domination of live reporting would not continue and that the second-guessers, theorists and bar-parlour military strategists would soon take control. The way they did so illustrated in a possibly alarming way the fact that most if not all journalists practising at the time had no memory of being involuntarily in the middle of an air raid, and had no idea that journalistic tricks – especially prophecy about what might happen next – could be dangerous to the lives of real people in a modern version of real war.

Of course, readers, listeners and viewers would at some stage want to know what was now likely to happen; but in a full-scale war they would have had to speculate among themselves rather than being fed information by the media that could be useful to the enemy.

Speculation about what military forces would go into an Afghanistan that was harbouring the terrorist Osama bin Laden, and what they would do when they got there was – to any reader who was old enough to remember the second world war – more like a script for the *Goon Show* than responsible journalism. It was also based, perhaps in this case fortunately, on very little precise information from those in the know. It was a trick to keep the readers, listeners and viewers interested, and, on behalf of newspapers, to maintain the rise in circulation that the disaster, and the public hunger for every word on it, had brought about.

Journalistic trickery, especially intelligent guesswork posing as information, was safe and well while many thousands of people in New York were not. To anyone with memories of the second world war from 1939 to 1945, including the closing down of the communist *Daily Worker* and the threatened closing down of the *Daily Mirror*, continuing stories about how the US had traced the suspected World Trade Center culprit, Osama bin Laden, from his satellite telephone had a surreal flavour.

Would you, in the name of journalistic frankness, let an enemy know that you had traced his satellite phone? The result was that Osama bin Laden stopped using that phone, which up to then had been monitored by Western intelligence services, and resorted to other means of communication, which could not be monitored.

Much the same sort of thing happened in the run-up to the Falklands war in 1982. British GCHQ had been monitoring telegrams to and from Argentina for several years, in highest secrecy. When the task force was due to set off for the Falkland Islands, Ted Rowlands, a former Minister of State at the Foreign Office, revealed in the House of Commons that this monitoring had been going on for many years. He declared that Argentina was, in security terms, an 'open book'.

The Argentinians immediately closed the book. They altered their codes, with the result that at the very time when the intelligence was most needed, the British were cut off from it. They could no longer plot where the two Argentinian submarines most dangerous to the task force were. In this case, journalists were only secondary culprits; the primary responsibility was at the door of the politician who had arguably opened his mouth too readily and too far in war conditions.

Because politicians in a democracy are sometimes naive, it does not follow that journalists can afford to be. In fact, wartime conditions do impose limits on what it is acceptable to report and comment on, and maybe they should. In democracies, criticizing the government is the old and honoured journalistic trick we know and, for most of the time, it can be constructive and good for the public as well as being 'good for sales'. As was demonstrated after 11 September 2001, war or near-war situations produce a sea change in the public mood, and what had seemed to be a harmless trick in days of peace could become highly objectionable in time of war.

One chat-show host in the USA criticized the repeated description of the World Trade Center attack as 'cowardly'. He argued that a suicide attack was brave and that Americans were cowardly when they fought battles by launching Cruise missiles when they were 2,000 miles away. Such was the tide of protest, and withdrawal of contracts by advertisers, that he was soon fighting to keep his job. Other commentators who did not adopt the American line totally were similarly attacked, including one who accused President George W. Bush of hiding in a hole in the ground – his secure shelter – immediately after the World Trade Center attack.

What would normally have been dismissed as merely the trick of claiming attention by going against the majority was now taken more seriously. Words really counted. Half a dozen words could be as explosive as a bomb or a hijacked aircraft. Journalists were, in general, being taken seriously in a way that should have given them pause: how did the public *usually* regard them? As wallpaper?

In a war, standard journalistic tricks can be threatening to life and morale, and are inevitably subject to restraint, voluntarily or otherwise. There is nothing automatically unethical about this and if there is non-acceptance or resistance on the part of journalists, that is possibly not because they are unpatriotic or obtuse, but simply too young to have experienced the realities and exigencies of wholesale war for themselves.

In the aftermath of the World Trade Center tragedy, as distinct from the time it took place, it was arguable that a lot of coverage was from comparatively young men and women who used some of the usual journalistic tricks without reference to the changed times.

At one point, just over a month after the destruction of the twin towers, speculation about what the anti-Osama bin Laden Alliance might do next, following the continual bombing of an Afghanistan which was sheltering him, had grown to such an extent that one of the only justifications possible for it was that it was deliberate disinformation that was being fed to the media to deceive the enemy. To anyone old enough to remember a 'real' war, it had a fantastical quality, and was as if President George W. Bush or Prime Minister Tony Blair had each invited bin Laden into their discussions.

There was a similar insensitivity on the morale front. Did not the media realize that broadcasting excerpts of a video that had apparently been made by Osama bin Laden before the

World Trade Center and Pentagon attacks would make the Alliance governments twitchy? Some sections of the media reminded us of the ruling in Britain in the past that IRA or Sinn Fein members' voices could not be broadcast but had to be dubbed by actors. This was widely seen as absurd at the time, and it was true that replacing Gerry Adams' voice with, say, Sir John Gielgud's, would have flattered the former and made him seem a much more appealing character.

But in the case of Osama bin Laden it was urged by Alliance governments that what he said could have contained code to instruct his followers to carry out other terrorist attacks. They urged that no further footage of Osama bin Laden should be broadcast. The request was ill-received. The Prime Minister called media heads into 10 Downing Street to explain the position further.

The difference between all these events and the sort of things that had happened in the second world war was conspicuous. In the first place, anyone who had suggested running footage of Hitler making a few of his best points in cinema newsreels – the primitive TV service available only in the London area had been suspended – would have been told to take two aspirins and lie down. It may be argued that openness has a value in society, even in a war, and that listening to Osama bin Laden would do more to turn audiences against him than anything else. But the fact that the argument that he might be broadcasting coded messages was resisted was more surprising. In the second world war, the very fact that it was suspected there might be hidden messages would itself have been 'hush hush', and all footage would have been inaccessible to anyone except perhaps the code-breakers at Bletchley Park.

Somewhere between the second world war and the destruction of the World Trade Center, the belief had grown up among journalists that even in a war they should be the sole arbiters of what should be published and what should not, even if, as the result of what was published, the politicians and the military had to change their war plans, or count their dead.

To the official mind journalists, apart from on-the-spot war correspondents, had acquired the trick of being, or trying to be, above the battle, of sitting comfortably on Cloud Nine while the world below writhed and died for their entertainment. To the journalistic mind, isn't a war just another story, to be judged by the same rules as applied in peacetime, while the politicians and the military are trying to play a trick on them and the public by limiting journalists' freedom?

The lack of major conflicts for over half a century had, by 11 September 2001 and beyond, produced a separation of viewpoints that must have seemed strange except to the elderly, but that had important implications for the democratic world. When and if the problem can be resolved may help determine the survival or disintegration of that world.

By the sixth week of the war on terror, all the common tricks of the journalistic trade were back again in full force.

When the Allied campaign in Afghanistan seemingly had become bogged down, bin Laden had predictably not been found or handed over, and the relentless bombing had had little apparent result other than to get the media as steamed up over six civilian deaths in Afghanistan as they had been over 3,000 deaths in New York, the phenomenon of the media biting their own national tail became even more visible. Criticism of the campaign from American and British sources reached such proportions that, in the absence of anything solid to report, the impression was that available space was being filled up with comment that must have struck those old enough to remember a 'real' war as surreal.

Some commentators put forward the 'anti-self-serving' view that what was appearing in the media was the result of their particular needs rather than devotion to any larger cause, the cause of truth included. The US Defence Secretary Donald Rumsfeld was said to hold over fifteen media briefings a *day*, which suggested the war was being run for the benefit of the media rather than the nation.

It was a reminder of the Falklands war when one correspondent actually told a government briefer, almost in so many words, that if they couldn't do better than he was doing, they really couldn't expect their wars to be covered in future.

The distinguished war correspondent Kate Adie put it neatly on the BBC Radio Sunday morning programme *Broadcasting House* just six weeks after 11 September. She said that the requirements of the 'affluent media' of the West meant that journalists constantly examined and criticized their own side because they had no access to the other side. This led to 'snapshots' of what was going on rather than a coherent picture, and leaders had to spend a large amount of time trying to meet media needs when they should have been doing something else. She was scornful of young correspondents who were more concerned about pushing themselves professionally than doing their jobs.

This was more than predictable mistrust, on the part of an older professional who had grown out of being pushy, of the younger professional who hadn't done so. It raised crucial questions about how tolerable journalistic tricks are in a situation that is important and life-threatening.

It is also a fair question to ask whether the trick of interpreting events not from the stance of an intelligent and humane person but from that of a coarser and dimmer observer soon crept back in sectors of journalism that were familiar with that demeaning perspective.

40

The Yob's Perspective

Journalists are apt to reason that politicians and other public figures have power over, or at least an influence on, the public and that therefore every aspect of their public and private lives should be open to inspection in a sophisticated democracy.

But, having made that declaration of their duty to a sophisticated public, they sometimes then go on to adopt the trick of inspecting politicians and other public figures not with the sophistication they have invoked, but from the perspective of a thick-skinned, simple-minded and coarse yob.

The politician with a mistress of long standing is not a man with complicated personal loyalties but a 'Wife-Cheating Rat', or 'Two-Timing Womanizer'. No matter that the wife is frigid and married the man for his money or position and that the mistress saved him from thoughts of suicide at a low period of his life. That would complicate the black and white melodrama, and might be beyond the comprehension of a yob. So it could not be told that way. That presumably is the patronizing reasoning.

The politician who kisses his secretary rather too vigorously in a House of Commons lift after the Christmas party becomes 'Randy Andy' or the 'Terror of the House'. It is a yob's view of his behaviour rather than an enlightened and educated one. It sees something as heinous when it may only be daft.

The female politician who is a single mother escapes rather more easily, partly out of chivalry and even more so because women are assumed to be politically correct in what they do or want to do. But she may still be open to the suggestion of child neglect if she runs foul of journalists for quite different reasons.

Similarly, there has lately been great public interest in whether politicians are gay or not. 'The Minister for Pickled Cucumbers is Gay!' 'The Shadow Minister for Silage is Gay!' Hold the front page! Try not to faint! There need not even be any sort of offence or impropriety involved.

All deviations from perfection are fair game. Even a politician with a bald head could find that his baldness was written about as if it were a grave offence instead of being a male secondary sex characteristic. Baldness is only a defect in an uneducated and unintelligent manual worker whose youth is his prime advantage on the labour market, and who is thus, poor fellow, the archetypal buyer of expensive baldness 'cures'. Attributing too much importance to whether a man is bald or not is not only trivial. It reveals a yob's perspective.

The point is not that all these facts are not of legitimate public interest: everything about politicians or the otherwise influential may be of interest to the public. It is that the way they are written or talked about by journalists sometimes does not even pretend to be sophisticated or definitive. The tone is often no better than that of the saloon or public bar bore who is best avoided, especially near closing time.

It has been argued that this way of writing about human behaviour is more 'accessible' than a more measured, a truly sophisticated approach; and that the pursuit of readers, listeners or viewers is not in itself a contemptible practice. Perhaps it isn't. But as a guide to how readers, listeners and viewers should react to what they are being told, it can be thoroughly misleading. It either blackens a human being who does not deserve it, or leaves the media 'consumer' unable to make his mind up about whether the person being described is an easy-going type who has strayed into personal difficulties, a cold and cynical manipulator of people, an irresponsible philanderer who is out of control in such a way as to be a menace in his job, an inveterate liar, or a man who has uncharacteristically gone off the rails in some way because of understandable circumstances.

In the cases already outlined, we have already seen that having a long-term mistress is open to various interpretations. It is not necessarily 'Minister Has Bit On Side'. Possibly it is, and he has another six lovers tucked away, one for each night of the week. However, it is equally possible that he regards himself as an independent and free agent because he and his wife have not got on well for years, though he will not divorce an uncongenial wife out of consideration for their children – which, if known, might make him a more acceptable figure.

The single-mother politician may be one of those women who should not be inflicted on any child: a careerist with no real maternal feelings. But equally she may be a loving mother who, despite her political duties, tries to give her children quality time and does not deserve to be attacked or lampooned.

As for the various ministers or Opposition spokesmen who are revealed to be 'gay', what does that actually mean? That they make themselves a nuisance by trawling public lavatories in search of poor, out-of-work adolescents? That they have made a vow of celibacy and sublimated their inconvenient sexual drives into doing work for the poor and needy? That they have a stable homosexual relationship? That they are perpetually juvenile in temperament but entirely blameless scout-masters?

The yob is not interested in such distinctions; and it is the yob's perspective that is sometimes presented by journalists who may not be yobs themselves but are struggling for conspicuous effect rather than sane and sensible analysis.

It may also be argued that journalists are not psychiatrists, doctors or nurses, and that they cannot be judges of the finer points of human behaviour. Maybe not. But ignorance cannot be pleaded as a justification for raucous over-simplification and coarse judgments. Journalists who ignore this precept tend to represent themselves as fearlessly exposing the 'hypocrisy' of the powerful to a public that ought to have a lower opinion of people with power than they have.

This can be bravado rather than candour. What simple-minded vulgarization of human behaviour may produce is less a reduction in trust between rulers and the ruled than a lurking feeling in the public mind that the politicians and other public figures concerned have been shabbily treated and probably do not deserve vilification, even if the public cannot resist reading about it. Thus, when there really *is* contemptible behaviour on the part of the powerful, the vocabulary for indicating its presence will have been exhausted.

In this connection, 'I don't know what to believe' is a sentiment heard time and time again from members of the public after reading or listening to the work of journalists. This public mistrust of anything said on the matter of human behaviour, this suspicion that every allegation is part of an all-embracing soap opera that can be enjoyed as fiction or semi-fiction, is as dangerous to democracy as the suppression of all private information about public people would be.

The adoption of the yob's perspective is a journalistic trick to produce folk yarns which does not 'help the people to decide'. It is a barrier to sophisticated human understanding, and may work against the revelation of real scandals which, when they occur, should most certainly be subjected to widespread journalistic examination and public scrutiny.

Playing on the heart-strings of the public as if they were the strings of a violin in a tragic operatic scene is another way of chronicling the world and the people in it that can be equally 'over the top'.

41

Distress

Writing about people in distress is a legitimate journalistic function. Burying the fact that what such people are really distressed about is being pursued by an aggressive posse of two dozen journalists is a journalistic trick of questionable validity.

A story might begin like this:

> Dabbing her streaming eyes and visibly trembling, the model Naomi Ferrari yesterday morning left the house of her lover, the clothes designer Raphael Fiat, in Chelsea.
>
> 'I do not know when or even whether I shall be returning,' she said. 'He has spent so much time on the Continent and I in Los Angeles that we have rarely been able to get together. Our divergent working schedules have put a heavy strain on our relationship.'

First, let us look at the tone of the alleged quotes. If the fictitious Naomi Ferrari really was dabbing her eyes and trembling, her quotes hardly fit: '... when or even whether I shall be returning' reads more like the words of a lawyer than those of a lovelorn and weeping woman. We can probably assume that a reporter asked her, 'When will you be returning?' and that she replied, 'I don't know.' Then the same reporter or a different reporter might have asked her, '*Will* you be returning?', to which she could have replied, 'I don't know.'

Neither does the sentence, 'Our divergent working schedules have put a heavy strain on our relationship', suggest spontaneity. It suggests either that she was fed the words by someone else, possibly her lawyer, or that she was asked, 'Have your divergent working schedules put a strain on your relationship?' and that she replied, 'Yes', or merely nodded her head.

But 'tailored' (that is, not necessarily invented) quotes have been dealt with elsewhere. In this case what is of interest is exactly *why* Naomi Ferrari was so upset that she was weeping and trembling. The answer emerges, through a careful sleight of hand, only towards the end of the story:

Swinging her handbag violently, Miss Ferrari swept past over fifty reporters, cameramen and film crews, crying, 'Leave us both in peace!'

The habit of journalists of writing about their own presence is a comparatively new phenomenon. They used to court anonymity. Each reporter wrote as if he were the only pebble on the news beach, and any suggestion that what was being said was influenced by the presence of large numbers of newsmen was therefore avoided. Often that is still true. But although journalists are reluctant to own up to the fact that their presence has conditioned the whole proceedings, whatever they are, they are sometimes eager to record the fact that they are there, as if it guarantees the importance of those proceedings.

The trick of using a news posse as a means of whipping up distress, that can then be reported upon, came about not perhaps as deliberate provocation but through the growth in the number of journalists turning out for 'important' stories, and their competitiveness.

At the turn of the millennium, many functions at local level – magistrate's courts, inquests, public dinners, hospital administration meetings – were no longer thought important enough to justify the presence (and the expense) of a reporter. But the presence of a national 'celebrity' was enough to unleash reporters from every conceivable sector of the national media. When the Beatles launched their Apple record-production company in offices off Baker Street in London in the 1960s, there were a handful of reporters. When Paul McCartney was married at Marylebone Town Hall some years later, there were more; but possibly only a quarter of the number of journalists who would turn up today for a similar event. And their presence would have been less obtrusive and their questions less prying.

In fact, at that time, a press posse was less likely, of itself, to cause distress. That massed journalists may help ruin a marriage or a relationship is convenient for journalists in search of an emotive story, but it is a trick of perspective. Real life can seldom be as fraught as when a hundred or more prying eyes and ears are concentrated on one spot, and that spot is you.

In local journalism, the one or two available reporters are often looked upon as friendly participants in events. In another context, a charging mob of competing journalists can be intimidating and amount to a trick, whether conscious or not, that distorts events and therefore distorts the truth.

Some journalists may like being part of an overpowering press pack and may even relish the rows they occasionally have with competing colleagues. If so, it is not the only sense in which journalists can enjoy a good row.

42

A Good Row

The public loves a good row. Or so journalists like to think. The fact that the people who are supposed to be rowing may sometimes hardly know one another, and may at most be irritated by each other's opinions, is sometimes disregarded – which can be a misleading trick.

The image propagated by journalists is often of a world full of people who are concerned only with their own ambitions, vanities and interests, and are touchily jealous of anyone they think possesses superior talents, and supercilious towards anyone they think possesses inferior ones. Such people are, of course, regarded as being always at one another's throats, or planning how they can be. Such a world view is depressing, but it is possibly thought to be good for circulation and viewing figures.

If the parties to the row stubbornly decline to settle their differences publicly – indeed, have to be reminded by reporters about what these differences are, since they are thinking about other things for most of the time – then they have to be provoked into anger, or have anger written into what they have said, possibly almost mildly, about one another.

The supposed fiery interfighting between cooks (I beg their pardon, chefs) may be a case in point. No doubt chefs can be temperamental, just as politicians, actors and even journalists can be from time to time. But if chefs like Jamie Oliver, Marco Pierre White and Gordon Ramsay were in reality as flurried by the existence of rival chefs as journalists sometimes like to imply, they would have succumbed to heart attacks, strokes or gastric ulcers years ago. If readers analyse closely their sayings about one another, they may detect that much of it amounts to versions of, 'I'm a better cook than he is': which is what every successful professional of any sort tends to believe, even if the shrewder ones mask it.

There is some bitchy pleasure to be extracted from men having a splat like ballerinas or washerwomen because of the entertaining loss of their macho dignity. But with the increasing presence and conspicuousness of women on the public stage, females are increasingly thought of as potential sources of public as well as private rudeness about one another.

Within weeks of the loss of over 3,000 lives in the terrorist destruction of the towers of the New York World Trade Center, which might have been thought of as encouraging a sense of proportion, large amounts of newspaper space were given to an alleged 'handbagging' between two media women, Esther Rantzen and Anne Robinson, each of whom was said to hate the other. The supposed hatred was based on the fact that Esther Rantzen was for many years the presenter of the *That's Life* television programme, in which her court of young males exposed scandals as well as carrots and potatoes with rude shapes. This was said to have earned her the title of the Queen of Corn. Whereas Anne Robinson had been for many years the presenter of the television game *The Weakest Link*, in which she made putting-down remarks to contestants who didn't know who Winston Churchill was, or who voted off those who were in fact the strongest contestants, or 'links', so that they themselves would have a better chance of winning, despite their own extensive ignorance. This was said to have earned her the title of the Queen of Mean.

When Anne Robinson published her autobiography, *Memoirs of an Unfit Mother*, in which she frankly revealed how at one point, years previously, her child had been removed from her care because of her excessive drinking, Esther Rantzen was asked by one daily newspaper, the *Daily Mail*, to review the book. Rantzen called Robinson a runaway success, which is not usually a term of abuse; but then said: 'How can the rest of us be pleased for her when she's so outrageously pleased with herself? The woman revealed in her autobiography is not a woman to envy.'

Quite: Anne Robinson had deliberately revealed her own days of suffering, which were followed by over twenty years in which she did not take a drink at all.

Esther Rantzen then suggested that Robinson's 'pulverizing the pathetic contestants' in *The Weakest Link* was a throwback to the mentality of her own mother, an overbearing woman who targeted the weak. And she suggested that, when Robinson was in charge of the *Watchdog* programme, executives had pleaded with her to be nicer to people. But she conceded that Robinson's pain was an element in her drive to succeed, and that without it she might lose the biting edge that made her unique.

It might be thought that, for an ambitious woman, Rantzen's views were judicious and expressed with moderation, and that many of them could have been accepted publicly by Robinson herself, whose autobiography did not lack frankness. But the review was written up in other sectors of the press as if there was a 'handbagging' going on, where a counter-handbag or even a nuclear explosion from Anne Robinson was imminent. It did not emerge.

The 'handbagging' was a 'good story'. However, as a reflection of what had been said and done it was probably much more hyperbolic than exact: it was an example of a journalistic trend where intellectual differences are personalized in such a way that those in the cheap seats can see plenty of blood, or a least tomato ketchup. As a conjuring trick of journalism, it may sometimes be thought to be too contrived to be convincing to intelligent readers.

But no doubt some journalists believe that, even if certain rows or alleged rows have less to them than meets the eye, readers will go on reading in the hope of one day encountering real blood. The weakness of that belief is that it is based on a single idea or premise: that the eminent in particular all hate one another and are sounding off against one another all the time, so that when one of them says 'Boo!' to another, it must be the sign of a long-disguised blood feud emerging.

There are other forms of journalism that are based on a single idea, but for reasons that do not involve blood sports. Brevity is one of them. These journalistic forms may not be consciously or unconsciously dishonest. But they may have disadvantages.

43

Single Idea

The journalist with a single idea – and that possibly hackneyed – has been introduced to us by television and radio, where even the most important events have to be described in very few words. There may be 200 words by way of a concise précis of the main point plus comment, rather than the 600, 800 or more words of a print report or article.

It may make for clarity, but it is at a price. The price is that a single hobby horse or cliché can take the place of a documented, reasoned explanation based on a number of points of view.

A newspaperman sits down in front of a keyboard, decides where and how his report will start, and goes on from his intro to defend its premises with facts, figures and quotes. Radio and television cannot carry too much in the way of facts and, especially, figures because, unlike when he is absorbing print journalism, these cannot be re-scrutinized on radio or television if the reader finds something unclear on first reading.

As newspapermen who have moved into radio or television have sometimes complained, they are too much in the hands of studio-bound presenters and producers. These functionaries, anxious to set the agenda themselves, sometimes practise the trick of bypassing all the research of the man on the spot and asking him a question for which he is not prepared, and which therefore produces a stutter, or a reply lacking in depth.

The man (or woman) on the spot defends himself against this by his own professional trick, assuming the glibness of a politician and adroitly bypassing the question by saying what he wanted to say in the first place. And, because he has to be clear in his mind before he goes on air, this will tend to be one idea, even if it is stated in different ways: he is not going to risk juggling with half a dozen, being nudged into unprepared waters by the presenter, and getting completely lost.

The radio and television influence, although it gives a sense of immediacy that print journalism cannot rival, can lead the journalist in the field into mechanical thinking and easily defended clichés rather than an exploratory state of mind. It is true that accomplished professionals like John Simpson or Kate Adie from the war zones, Andrew Marr from the political front and Peter Jay from the economics front, have used their authority on television to propound facts and express views that may go against the grain. But that could be because their authority has been deployed in preparing those back at base before they go on air, so that they have a comparatively free run in relation to what they want to say.

Print journalism unconsciously gears itself up to aping the electronic media while at the same time trying to carve out an impregnable current and future role for itself that television and radio cannot hope to usurp. This it does by providing readers with opinion articles of between 1,000 and 1,500 words, often written by highly intelligent people like Simon Jenkins (who once in his column propounded the admirable view that the true marvel of durable communication, the book, should have come *after* the invention of the computer, and therefore have been rightly regarded by everyone as better and more up to date), Libby Purves and Matthew Parris of *The Times*, Peter Preston of *The Guardian*, Melanie Phillips of the *Daily Mail* or, on a more humorous front, Oliver Pritchett of *The Sunday Telegraph* – all of them writers worth reading irrespective of whether you agree or not with their views or slant, none of them being the prisoner of predictable formulas. But equally often, in less perceptive hands, such opinion pieces are predictable variations on a single idea, that single idea being to recycle received wisdom, left of centre, right of centre or whatever, rather than to present new perceptions.

Those print journalists who – all honour to them – try to avoid this trap can fall into another one by adopting the trick of finding out what most commentators are saying and then writing their piece from a diametrically opposite point of view. If most people are saying that the Dome at Greenwich was a national disgrace that made Britain a laughing stock of the new millennium, they would argue that, on the contrary, the Dome is an essay in popular culture that should define it. If most commentators are saying that industrial and individual pollution is causing global warming and helping to destroy the world, they will claim that this is superstitious nonsense, and that cosmic forces making for global warming are far more powerful than the effects of the factory by the river, or granny's aerosol.

Such positions can be merely perverse rather than revealing. But they are sometimes forced onto print journalism as a trick with which radio and television cannot easily compete: a 1,500-word feature or opinion column would take more than fifteen minutes to read out, and the attention span of the radio and television audience, even for material prophesying the end of the world, would be considerably less than that.

It is true that splurges of opinion of this type may play a useful purpose in getting subjects aired. But the general reader should always bear in mind the professional needs of this sector of the media when he asks himself how much attention he should pay to what is written. Is he the victim of a professional trick? Was the journalist performing variations on one idea, and that possibly concocted to be provocative, or was he truly extending the argument?

One talented radio and television commentator, Jeff Randall, who had been working for newspapers, was told by a newspaper acquaintance, Piers Morgan, then editor of the *Daily Mirror*, when he started working at the BBC, that to be successful in his new career as a broadcaster he should learn to be 'more tabloid'. Just so. The essence of radio and television is indeed to adopt the trick of thinking simply, preferably in terms of a single idea. But the listener, viewer and reader is well advised to think all the time about the implications of that. And in relation to all such journalism he is wise to ask: is this an exercise in thinking or a trick based on a cliché or on attitudinizing?

It is said that every picture tells a story and, in journalism, that a picture can sometimes tell it better than hundreds or thousands of words. But pictures can be made to deceive through the trick of accompanying words, so that the picture 'shows', not what it does show, but what the words say it does.

44

Picture Versus Story

The great suspense-film director Alfred Hitchcock used to claim that the same shot of an actor wearing a slight smile could be used to imply practically *any* feeling, depending on the shots immediately before it. If you preceded the shot of the actor's face with that of a pretty girl undressing by a window across the street, the expression became a lascivious leer. If you preceded it with the shot of a car crash, the expression would be one of pained horror. If it were preceded by a picture of an attractive baby, then the expression would become dotingly indulgent. And all with precisely the same shot of the actor's face.

Similarly, pictures in newspapers and magazines are sometimes arbitrarily chosen to support a thesis: that the particular individual is happy, miserable, satisfied, frustrated, in the peak of ecstasy or suffering agonies from a scandal involving him. It is said that the camera cannot lie. In fact the pictures used can easily mislead in relation to what is being claimed or argued in the text of a story; sometimes they could equally well be used to illustrate the very opposite. It is a journalistic trick that repays watching. Any exaggeration or hype in the text or picture caption can thus be detected.

The journalist Harold Evans, a former editor of *The Sunday Times*, once remarked acutely: 'The camera cannot lie. But it can be an accessory to untruth.'

Examples are not difficult to find. A few weeks after the 2001 terrorist attack on the USA, one newspaper carried on its front page a picture of the British Prime Minister Tony Blair on his return to London after the 40,000 miles he had travelled in the course of interviewing overseas leaders in an effort to expand the Coalition against international terrorists. The headline was one word: 'Shattered'.

To support and justify this version of the state he was in, his picture should perhaps have shown him cross-eyed, dribbling from a strawberry-red nose, unshaven and with his shirt-tail hanging out. In fact, it showed nothing of the kind. If you had seen the picture without the story, the reader would never have dreamed that the Prime Minister was anything other than a man, any man, who had just had a long air journey and was thinking hard about something or other.

The only signs that he was 'shattered' were that (a) the end of his shirt collar was projecting half an inch from his jacket in a way that collars are apt to do if a necktie has been readjusted without the benefit of a mirror; (b) about half a dozen hairs over his forehead looked as if they had not been freshly brushed; (c) he had traces of bristles on his face, as may happen to men on long flights; and (d) his nose was slightly red, as with many people who step off a heated aircraft into the chill British climate.

In the absence of anything better, the picture could have been used to reinforce a story called 'PM Concentrates on Serious Problems'; 'Tony Blair Wonders What to Buy His Wife for Her Birthday'; 'PM After Committing Ten Serial Killings'; 'PM Relieved to be Home'; 'Tony Blair Withstands 40,000 Miles Without Turning a Hair'; 'PM Forgets his Comb and Razor', or, since he was shown wearing an Armistice Day poppy, 'PM Decently Makes Time to Think of the Fallen of Two World Wars'.

Every picture tells a story. But, if you look closely, it may not be the one accompanying it. Even if it does suit the story being illustrated, it may have been taken when the person's mood had nothing to do with it. The 'agonized' face of someone involved in an alleged scandal may have been the result of the man in the picture stubbing his toe while getting out of a car.

Tears may have been caused by a very cold day. The 'Brave Widow Refuses to Cry' may be wishing that her husband had died earlier. 'The Star Who Laughs Off Sex on Aircraft' allegations may have been laughing hysterically because she felt persecuted.

The camera may not lie, but its products, when used in conjunction with stories, may occasionally mislead. If they mislead intentionally, as for instance if they show a politician or other celebrity laughing at his child's funeral without explaining that he was laughing at the antics of his younger children who were trying to cheer him up, that would indeed be a trick, and one that could have legal consequences.

It would be a noticeable rarity. It can be for accidental reasons that a picture lies because of the words used with it. *The Guardian* is the pioneer of an enlightened and useful device, the readers' editor and his column in which readers' complaints can be dealt with intelligently in a way that treats them with respect as human individuals, and can give them an apology where it is due.

On 10 July 2006, the readers' editor Ian Mayes discussed a complaint from an England football supporter who had been pictured by an agency photographer wearing a white German army-style helmet while he was in Germany for the World Cup. The picture, illustrating a story about uncouth British football fans, was used with a caption (not the agency photographer's) that described the supporter's helmet as 'Nazi-style headgear', when in fact it was army-style and not specifically Nazi. The reader claimed that he was made to look as if he was one of those uncouth England supporters the story was complaining about, and received an apology.

If the camera can be made to lie about human identity and mood through the use of words, whether accidentally or not, words can be equally misleading when describing other aspects of human behaviour, or alleged human behaviour, that include such novelettish concepts as the often reported act of 'snubbing', which occurs frequently if some headlines are to be believed.

45

'Snubbed'

When Prince Charles and Camilla Parker Bowles had, for legal reasons, to hold their civil wedding in Windsor Register Office in the Guildhall, rather than in Windsor Castle a few yards away, the Queen announced that she would not attend it, although she would attend the Church of England blessing afterwards and host the reception. Newspapers were full of the question of whether the Queen was 'snubbing' her son and Mrs Parker Bowles.

No, she was not doing that: at least, not unless she and her advisers had suddenly lost their wits. So visible a snub would be dangerous for the institution of the monarchy as well as an offence to any mother's heart. Snubs are a hazardous business in any public context, for they unnecessarily pile up future re-venge and other trouble. They belong more to television soap-operas like *EastEnders* or *Dallas* than to real public life.

In this case, those who spoke for the Queen made it clear that she would not attend the wedding in a public place be-cause she did not wish to create a media circus in such a pub-lic place. It might have been assumed that that would be the end of the matter. The assumption would have been wrong because, for days afterwards, newspapers had a field day speculating about the 'snub', and turning over the question of whether there had been one.

It was a typical trick from journalists with pages to fill: first suggest a dubious motive, and then speculate at length about whether it existed or not. At least the London *Evening Standard* of 18 March 2005 had made up its mind about Prince Charles's father Prince Philip's decision to go ahead with an overseas trip during the week his son got married. A screamer front-page heading, covering most of the page, pro-claimed: 'PHILIP'S WEDDING SNUB TO CHARLES'. This was backed up by quotes from a 'senior royal source' which said that it could not be 'guaranteed' that Prince Philip would return in time.

The only positive statement about what the Prince would and would not do was that he would not attend the register office wedding, but would attend the service of dedication and the reception at Windsor Castle afterwards – just like the Queen. Was this a snub? A snub is a deliberate attempt to insult someone by not doing something one would normally be expected to do. There was nothing 'normal' about the unique Charles-Camilla wedding, and that made it difficult to say what was a snub and what was not. Obviously, a snub makes a better story than a non-snub. But seeing a snub at every juncture in public affairs can amount to a journalistic trick.

In this case, when no explicit evidence was likely to be found – in the sense of Prince Philip ringing up newspapers and saying, 'Here's a good story for you. I am snubbing my son and that woman, whatever her name is!' – one has to ask whether the inferences were justified. Certainly, the fact that Prince Philip was not going to the register office wedding did not necessarily indicate a personal snub because he was merely following the sovereign's own decision. But for a spokesman to say that the Prince might not be returning to this country early enough to attend the wedding of his son? Surely, for someone in Prince Philip's position to say anything but, 'I shall certainly make it my business to be back in time,' is saying in effect, 'I have more important priorities than my son and the future monarch's wedding'? This is the sort of analysis that could go on for many column inches.

But although in individual cases the suggestion of a snub may be reasonable, rather than an over-dramatizing trick, certain 'snubs' do strain credibility. To judge from some heavy-breathing journalism, the world is a magnified soap-opera in which people spend their entire lives flouncing and denouncing, fighting and slighting, blubbing and snubbing.

There is no doubt that that last word is over-worked in some journalism. Can the trick be a legitimate, even a valuable one? Yes, if it is based on a real possibility as distinct from a manufactured one. But if it is a matter of an Aunt Sally being set up so that it can be knocked down, it is a trick that is only marginally and tangentially informative at best, and tastelessly and cruelly entertaining at worst.

According to the apparent philosophy of those who employ it, if one picks up and reads Jeffrey Archer's *First Among Equals* one has 'snubbed' his *Twelve Red Herrings*. If one has gone with an estate agent to look over two houses, and buys one of them, one has 'snubbed' the owner of the other. If one goes into a supermarket and buys a bottle of Italian wine, one has 'snubbed' the English wine, and the French, Californian, Australian, Portuguese, Chilean, Argentinian, New Zealand and Hungarian wines, too. If one has bought the wine at Sainsbury's, then one has snubbed Tesco, Waitrose, Asda and Morrison's, and so on.

How can this be? The answer is simple. It can't. It is a transparent trick, at least in the eyes of watchful and perceptive people, to concoct a colourfully dramatic conflict or a cauldron of ill-will where possibly none exists.

Nor are tabloid newspapers the sole culprits. One magazine for writers once led its front page with the heading: 'BBC Snubbed over Youth Channel'. From this you might assume that the government had told the BBC: 'Your plans for a youth channel are pathetic, especially as you have not got sufficient talent to serve your existing television stations. Get lost!'

The facts did not bear out this interpretation. What had happened was that the government had rejected the BBC's application for a new digital youth channel to replace *BBC Choice*. All the rest of the BBC's digital proposals, including those for two children's channels, were accepted. Did the Director-General of the BBC, Greg Dyke at the time, express resentment at being 'snubbed' by the government? He did not. He said merely that he was 'surprised and disappointed', not that he had been snubbed and was therefore incandescent with rage, foaming at the mouth, rending his garments and contemplating fire-bombing Downing Street.

'I have given the BBC a chance to create high quality, home-grown programmes,' announced the Culture Secretary Tessa Jowell at a Royal Television Society meeting in Cambridge. 'In particular, I believe the new stations for children offer the hope of a new golden age of children's programmes; a real national asset which will become a lasting legacy for children and their parents.'

Some snub. The fact was that four main proposals had been put forward by the BBC and three were accepted with the enthusiasm that the minister hinted at. Snub? Why not 'blood feud'? To suggest that the outcome of the BBC's talks with the government at this time were anything more than an illustration of the fact that, in any negotiation, you get some things you want but not others, is to bend words into near meaninglessness.

But the trick or the sincere but deluded process of seeing snubs where none necessarily exist is far from unusual. Any violent or semi-violent word in a newspaper or magazine heading should be taken with a pinch of salt unless and until it has been plainly and soundly backed up by the story that follows it, or by stories elsewhere.

Fine distinctions about shades of meaning are unfortunately becoming more difficult to convey. It was always difficult to convey them in tabloid newspapers, but over the past decade or so broadsheet newspapers have increasingly taken on board the practices of the tabloids: in headings, in first paragraphs and sometimes in the whole content of stories. Purists might argue that we no longer have broadsheets in the sense of the word twenty or thirty years ago, let alone in the days when *The Times* had only a grey mass of classified advertisements on its front page ...

46

The Disappearing Broadsheet

The broadsheet newspaper *The Independent* may have started more than it bargained for when it led the way to 'tabloidism' by converting itself physically into a tabloid format. Other broadsheets soon followed.

The Times first gave its readers the choice of a broadsheet or a tabloid version, presumably to point them persuasively in the direction of the tabloid, and then offered the tabloid alone.

At one stage, *The Guardian* and *The Daily Telegraph*, at opposite political poles, were for a time the national dailies (excluding the more specialized *Financial Times*) that stuck to the broadsheet size. *The Guardian* then moved to a slightly larger tabloid presentation, in the 'Berliner' size.

Does the size of a tabloided newspaper *merely* make it easier for readers to read on commuter trains without damage to their elbows? Or does it, perhaps at a subliminal level, affect its approach to news? There is a case for the latter supposition. A tabloid newspaper page is easy to make arresting by the use of very short news stories with punchy headings arranged with some sense of priorities. A tabloid page designed like this with shortish stories looks rather like a broadsheet page whose longer stories can be laid out with the same sense of priority and visual rhythm. But a former broadsheet featuring commendably long stories on tabloid-sized pages may find itself running page after page with one story, or two at most per page, all the pages looking rather alike and so being apt to send the reader to sleep or to disorientate him: where *is* he in the paper now? – the home news pages, the overseas news pages, the features pages, or the financial pages?

This technical fact, allied to a tendency among contemporary newspapers to strain for entertainment rather than the communication of information, can lead to 'tabloidization' in more than format. There were indications before the tabloidizing battle began in earnest that some of the broadsheet press was turning tabloid in a psychological sense, too, which smoothed the way for the tabloid format. The Afghan city of Konduz was under siege by the fragmenting Northern Alliance warlords on 23 November 2001, as part of the campaign against sheltered terrorists that was undertaken after the destruction by terrorists of the twin towers of the World Trade Center in New York. One newspaper ran the headline: 'City of Blood and Betrayal'. Which tabloid newspaper was this? It wasn't a tabloid at all but one of the most historically respected broadsheets, *The Times*.

Or should one say 'most historically respected former broadsheets'? For although some newspapers are indeed printed as broadsheets in size, many if not most of them can be considered as at least partly tabloidized as they strive for sensational effects instead of reporting events in a cool and measured way.

Does it matter? Is a tabloid the same as a broadsheet newspaper except that it says the same things in a punchier way with shorter words, sentences, paragraphs and stories? That used to be true, but it is doubtful whether it is still true to the same extent. Thirty or forty years ago, journalists on daily tabloids, which then meant the *Daily Mirror* to all intents and purposes, were rather similar to their brothers on 'serious' newspapers. By the 1980s they had become quite dissimilar, the broadsheet journalist still going for the essence of a story, while the tabloids searched out sexual scandal and human aberrations of all types. Perhaps feeling themselves threatened by the tabloids, the broadsheets first began to raise their voices and lower their language and coarsen their attitude, and then imitated the format of tabloids whose philosophy they had partly absorbed.

The difference between an intelligent broadsheet (or former broadsheet) journalist and a tabloid journalist, it could be argued, is that a broadsheet journalist conducts a conversation with readers of equal intelligence to his own, whereas an intelligent tabloid journalist concocts a sensation for people of lesser intelligence to marvel at. In other words, the broadsheet journalist is, or should be, conversing with his equals, while a tabloid journalist is prescribing from an intellectual distance what he thinks should be prescribed for the delectation of people who are not as smart as he is. But one has to ask whether journalists on the broadsheets, or former broadsheets, now think in the same terms as their headings and their intros in their off-duty lives.

Broadsheets of fifty years ago, such as *The Times* with its small classified advertisements on page 1, and *The Daily Telegraph*, with its unsensational presentation of sensational court stories, may look dull to the modern eye. But at the time, all broadsheets were almost blindly trusted by their readers, to an extent not seen today, when broadsheets and ex-broadsheets resort to snappy headings, labouring-the-point intros, strenuous puns, irrelevant innuendo and mildly pornographic pictures.

The commercial calculation that inspired the disappearance of the old-fashioned broadsheet is not encouraging. It presumably was that sober broadsheets appeal to intelligent people and that, in any society, they are in a minority. There are, as we have seen when discussing 'Dumbing Down', more readers, listeners and viewers who are not intelligent than there are would-be readers, listeners and viewers for intelligent material, plainly presented. And there are thus greater profits to be made from them.

Because majorities now dictate *taste* as well as political policies, hence the disappearance of the once invariable necktie, even intelligent journalists may have a vested interest in not appearing so. Intelligent 'consumers' are under pressure not to appear intelligent – certainly not to flaunt their intelligence publicly by reading a newspaper without pretty pictures. It became more fashionable for a banker to read *The Sun,* the *Daily Mirror* or *Daily Star* than it would be for a train driver to read *The Times, The Guardian* or *The Daily Telegraph.*

If this analysis was perceived by the broadsheets to be correct, the trick for them was to present themselves in such a way that they could not be rejected as 'elitist', meaning in this instance intelligent, but would have to be considered 'accessible' to a wider range of readers, which in practice meant whether intelligent or not. Like all tricks, it had a price, which was a certain mistrust among those intelligent readers, especially older ones who could remember pre-1980s broadsheets, but whose doubts could be ignored because they would inevitably be replaced as readers by new, if less intelligent, ones.

The Independent was an attempt to create a genuine broadsheet that was attached to no political party view and really *was* intelligently independent. It was ironic, therefore, that it became the first of the broadsheets to introduce a tabloid version of itself, which achieved some success. It was as if readers were now insisting on newspapers not only being tabloid in thought but also in format.

Whether in the long term the trick of tabloidizing broadsheets will staunch falling circulations in the industry generally, or dig a final grave for this form of newspaper, has yet to be established. In the meantime, intelligent readers of tabloidized broadsheets may regrettably be tempted to apply to them some of the caution they might apply when reading the traditional tabloids. That old adage, 'Never believe anything you read in the newspapers', could even come to apply to those newspapers who might once have been exempted from it. Let us hope not, but (in real terms) it is money rather than intelligent, high-standard journalism that has the most powerful disciples.

I apologize for that bracketed phrase. It came to mind as easily as any other cliché, but I have allowed it to stand for reasons that will now be explained.

47

In Real Terms

If you find any journalist – or, for that matter, anyone else – using the expression 'in real terms', ask yourself what the reality being invoked actually is. Suspect a trick.

The phrase is too useful to would-be deceivers and in too constant use for it ever to pass unchallenged. For what are we to assume by it? We are to assume that the rest of the world is deceived by all sorts of wrong ways of looking at the issue in question; but that the writer or speaker is uniquely endowed with unchallengeable facts, or with messages from the Almighty, so that he can show you the issue is not as you thought it was but is something else 'in real terms', when in fact the issue may remain precisely as you thought it was.

The phrase was increasingly used from the time of the 1970s inflation. It may be acceptable to say that a suit bought for £30 in 1960 would 'in real terms' be selling for £600 by the twenty-first century. But even here the phrase adds nothing to 'a suit bought for £30 in 1960 would be selling at £600 by the twenty-first century'. The introduction of the phrase 'in real terms' is usually more deceitful than this: it can be no more than an attempt to lend an aura of hypnotic undeniability to what is just a proposition or an argument.

When the sums are larger, or the social, political or sporting factors more extensive, the use of the phrase can be still more dubious. Suppose that you read a story whose intro is similar to this:

> The government has the reputation of being competent in the management of the economy, and has had several years with a growing gross national product, but in real terms its record has been abysmal.

Here we are being asked to doubt the usual measure of financial well-being, an improved balance of payments, and to agree that in spite of achieving this, a government's record has been 'abysmal'. It is a big step, and a trick is needed to make it work: in this case the use of the 'in real terms' cliché. This trick implies that despite the good bits, there are bad bits that are somehow of more 'real' significance. Maybe it is being implied that although the government has balanced the books, it has neglected other matters that are just as important: education, the social services, the health services?

In that case, the intro should in honesty have been:

> The government has the reputation of being competent in the management of the economy but, it was claimed yesterday, only at the cost of neglecting necessary expenditure on public services.

This makes the point specific. It sets it out honestly, without the aid of propaganda implying that there are mysterious 'real' rules out there which are agreed by all, and judged against which the government would be seen as failing. Who is a journalist to say in a report what are 'real' considerations and what are not real? It begs too many questions. The journalist should report what is going on as specifically as he can and refrain from slipping in opinions on what factors are more 'real' than others. Even if he is reporting a speech, and quotes the speaker as using the 'real terms' phrase, he should follow it in his report with a defence, if there is one, of the assertion that virtues are being undermined in the 'real' world by sins of its opponents.

In real terms, Gordon Brown had no chance in the 1990s of becoming PM.

Here the trick suggests that Gordon Brown and his supporters have been putting it about that Gordon Brown should have been Leader of the Labour Party but were pipped at the post at the last minute by the Tony Blair campaign. Under some mysterious higher law of probability, he was never anywhere near being a candidate for the leadership of the Labour Party and thus Prime Minister after a Labour Party general election victory. The implication is that he was ill-equipped and unsuited, all of this through the use of 'in real terms'. What *actually* happened later could demolish this 'reality'.

In the sporting field, also, the phrase must be watched carefully:

> Though he has recently made some very spectacular saves, in real terms he can no longer be regarded as a good goalkeeper, and is past his best.

Unless the subsequent part of the report can document that assertion, the reader is here being asked to cast aside the usually accepted idea of the chief quality of a goalkeeper – his ability to prevent goals being scored – in favour of some mysterious and unstated 'real' criteria. The man does all that can be asked of any goalkeeper but is in some way unsatisfactory. He is, by way of a defence of this premise, stated to be 'past his best', presumably because he has reached some arbitrary age band. Even a man who is in indisputable fact 'past his best', but who can still save goals better than the opposition, is a better proposition than a younger man who is less good at saving goals. The reader here is asked to believe the reverse of the truth: 'in real terms' a man is to be judged by his age rather than by his performance.

Or suppose we had:

> David Beckham and his wife Victoria Beckham have been hailed as akin to the royal family in the public mind, but in real terms they are less than that.

Doubtless the royal family will still be around in some shape or form when temporary celebrities are no more. Doubtless being a monarch requires a shrewd grip on statecraft that would elude most people who spend their lives wearing silly clothes when cameras are around. But all the same, in fairness to 'Becks and Spice', it should be made clear in any report why they are to be regarded as being no royal family. It is not enough to say that 'in real terms' they are no royal family without saying what those terms are. You cannot put a person in their place without saying what that place is. It is not enough to say that, despite most indicators of success, they are in higher, nobler, more sensible 'real' terms to be considered as failures.

In arts coverage you might come across this:

In real terms, Simon Callow is an unsatisfactory successor to Sir John Gielgud.

In the arts, reputations are apt to be as fluid as they are in politics or sport. 'Real' criteria are difficult to find and are always open-ended when found. Why is it necessary to compare Simon Callow with Sir John and to imply that if there was a contest on the theatrical equivalent version of a level playing field – which there could never be – Mr Callow would be in some way unsatisfactory?

More to the present point, why is it necessary to imply that there are 'real' criteria in the arts, as compared with the subjective criteria that all intelligent people know are the only ones that can be applied to the arts, and that in relation to these Simon Callow is to be found wanting in a way Sir John would not have been?

Always suspect that if 'real' terms are being invoked, the *actual* terms being implied though not stated would *not* be as conclusive as the journalist might hope. It may be a sign that a journalist is bored with writing about the same limited range of personalities, and inclined to put the boot in for insubstantial reasons.

48

Same Old Celebrities

The obituarist's art has been described as that of making a reader interested in the death of a man or woman we have never heard of. Phil Osborne, the obituaries editor of *The Guardian*, has written in *The Guardian Book of Obituaries* of the need to create reader interest by producing a rounded picture of people's lives, achievements, disappointments and failures.

The trick of writing interestingly about *anybody*, alive or dead, is to combine a ferret's nose for human interest with perception, humanity, humour, irony if need be, and a view of entertainment that does not insult the intelligence of the reader.

If a journalist or his office superiors lack such ability, it is much easier to cycle and recycle the 'same old gang of "celebrities"' on every other page of a newspaper or magazine, their names alone being considered to be sufficient bait. In particular, it is much easier for gossip column editors to ask for paragraphs about that same old gang who they think will catch the reader's eye – and for the lazy interviewer who prefers swotting up on a member of the gang in the cuttings library. Hence the popularity of this trick, which leads directly to a huge amount of intrusive coverage and insensitive treatment of that gang, at any particular time, of celebrities and 'celebrities'.

Gossip columns have changed in recent years. They used to introduce readers to a medley of extraordinary folk, and they might be able to do so again if writers and readers tended not to be lazy, preferring clichés about the old gang to something and someone newer.

In practice, however, the reader is now more likely to look at the gossip column of even a 'quality' newspaper and find that the Prime Minister, the minister most in the news at that particular moment and the same old sportsmen and women are mentioned in two or three out of the six paragraphs comprising the column.

This trick could strike some readers as being journalistic soap-opera at its most vapid and its laziest. It encourages an inward-looking attitude to life. While television tries to appeal to its audiences with programmes on what the universe was like fifty million years ago, the world of newspapers and magazines often limits itself to producing infinite variations (if not the same variations) on half a dozen people who happen to be the 'celebrities' of the moment: in other words the people at whom most cameras happen to be pointing.

No doubt it would be claimed that 'the readers want it, because if they didn't, it wouldn't sell newspapers'. This argument, even if true, is confronted by the law of diminishing returns. The fewer the personalities the reader meets on the printed page, the more limited his interests become, the less he is encouraged to look for a world outside the introverted media village populated by a few people who *may* have some tangible ability but may simply be people it is convenient for the cameras to focus on because they are not likely to assault the cameraman or sue the reporter. Laziness in the journalist and the reader can march hand in hand.

If two 'celebrities' can be found who are in a relationship that can be described, misdescribed, analysed, misanalysed and exaggerated every day, so much the better. Does this apply only to the tabloid press and the sort of misbehaving actors and models it loves to publicize? Unfortunately it no longer does.

Take as an example the relationship during the later period in office of the Labour government of the 2000s between its leader Tony Blair and the Chancellor of the Exchequer, Gordon Brown. It was the subject of variations in the 'quality' as well as the tabloid press and other scandal sheets. The facts were that originally Brown apparently expected to be given the leadership of the Labour Party, but that after the sudden and unexpected death of the party leader John Smith he was overtaken by a groundswell, concocted or not, in favour of Tony Blair. Blair had fewer enemies, was the better PR manipulator and had a family which at the time Brown did not, all making him easier to sell to the electorate than Gordon Brown.

When Tony Blair came to power, Brown was immediately made Chancellor of the Exchequer. Both plainly needed each other, but relations between them were predictably subject to ups and downs. In short, any journalist who didn't know what

to write about was tempted to write about Blair-Brown relations, especially when prodded by the PR machines on either
side.

The fact that even politicians who hate one another can
work together for years if their interests dictate it, was largely
ignored in favour of soap-opera variations. The feeling of
Brown that he had been cheated of the leadership, and the feeling of Blair that he had better watch his back, were stock
ingredients for a continuing saga that ran and ran like *The
Archers*, *Coronation Street* or *EastEnders*.

The Blair-Brown relationship was the subject of daily speculation that was either based on, or dressed up as, inside knowledge. Writing about it was easier than finding out things of
more direct relevance to the country. The trick was to dress up
speculation or spin from one side as insider fact, and to rely on
the supposition that almost any allegation or theory would be
difficult, or impossible, to disprove – not least because no one
would be likely to believe the denials of any politician.

This situation, which was of great value to those wishing to
employ journalistic tricks, was irritating to the politicians, who
increasingly sought to limit journalists' scope. They did this
not by withholding information but by 'spinning' it to journalists in such a way and in such a volume that they would almost
become mere carriers of 'spin' that they dared not ignore. Investigative journalism was simply drowned in a flood of spoon-
fed 'stories'.

This happened essentially because the habit of writing about
a limited number of 'names', in politics or anywhere else,
sometimes in intrusive and casually abusive terms, had become
endemic. It fostered parochial, easy journalism which in turn
encouraged an addiction to abuse and laziness in the reader.
It is an easy trick that largely bypasses intelligence and leads,
not to enthusiasm for genuinely probing journalism, but to the
peril of becoming addicted, not to what is necessary or desired,
but to prattle about the same small, if changing, gang of
people that easily fills the pages of newspapers and magazines.

Addiction, even to a simple trick, is not a life-enhancing condition. Neither, for that matter, is journalistic incitement to the
reader, listener or viewer to regard money matters as the most

important topic of all to hear about in relation to human beings.

<h1 style="text-align:center">49</h1>

Money Worship

The £8 million centre-forward Jethroe passed a terrific cross, which was however intercepted for the opposition by the £9 million goalkeeper Pethroe. Soon after, United's new £10 million signing, Tescoe, scored.

What sort of game is being played here? Football or money worship? What trick is being played? Undoubtedly the worship of money is the whole of society's problem rather than journalists' exclusive responsibility. But by espousing it so frequently, and often so irrelevantly and so crudely, journalists may help to intensify it.

The degree to which society has accepted the view that money has magical qualities, and that its owners and manipulators are high priests of a religion, is both depressing and, in terms of our society and civilization, pathetic. It is expressed in many ways. The compensation culture is one of the most insidious: people thinking it clever, and indeed in line with some sort of new morality, to sue for money for the slightest real or imagined injury or injustice. It is as if physical contact with a sum of money will cure all the heart's and the mind's ills, much as earlier generations believed that touching sacred relics would have similar beneficial effects.

A wife loses her husband in a ghastly accident at work, and sues her employers for compensation. If the husband was the principal bread-winner, it is true that, if the firm were at fault, they might be expected to compensate her for this loss of income. In almost every other respect, a sum of money can be about as relevant to the sufferings of the bereaved as rubbing oneself with a fake sacred relic would be.

Remove the issue of loss of income from the calculation. A high income husband who loses his wife will miss a human being. What good will a sum of money do in relation to that? He is sorry that her children have lost a loving mother. Will a large sum of money replace her? It could be argued that by bringing a legal action, the husband would be attempting to keep his wife alive in his own eyes, or at least attempting to retain a link with his wife. But few widowers would put themselves through an expensive legal action because of such a feeling: money is the magical substance that is sought because of the perhaps unconscious belief that contact with it can work miracles.

The same philosophy lies behind the habit of journalists seeking out and revealing the value of the house owned by a person who is being interviewed or described:

> The folk-singer Sam Salmon stood on the front doorstep of his £2,500,000 house yesterday and said that his relationship with the exotic dancer Funny Bunny had broken up, and that she had set off in her £200,000 Rolls Royce to her own £3,000,000 mews house in Kensington.

What was that? A journalist's report or an auctioneer's valuation? You will see this trick pulled in several newspapers practically every day. The people concerned don't much like it – it gives too much of a guiding light to burglars – but put up with it because it flatters them, unless the estimates are too low, in which case they might be tempted to sue on the grounds of defamation in a society that equates wealth with virtue.

The nature of a religion may be judged to some extent by its high priests. Who are the true high priests of present-day society? Not the leaders of the Church of England, of whom fewer people seem to take notice. Not the priests at street level, who are sometimes considered figures of fun. No, the high priests are the heads of vast corporations, manipulators of money. Or merchant bankers, manipulators of money. Or newspaper proprietors who have never been journalists in their lives, manipulators of money. Or even the bureaucracy which has taken over public management of the arts.

This state of affairs is reflected, magnified and reinforced by journalists writing with the unspoken assumption that such people are those who matter most.

Thirty years ago, for instance, media coverage in newspapers consisted mainly of reports about artists who appeared on radio and television. It was possible to read it without revulsion or yawning because the personalities were of some interest and their acts were known to the public. Now most of the media coverage is about the executives of radio and television stations, in effect manipulators of money again. A great deal of the material that appears in the Media pages of general newspapers might be thought to belong more to the Financial pages, unless you believe that the acting in the boardroom may well be of a better quality than the acting that features in the television company's drama productions.

The fact is that people who can accumulate money are often ungifted in any other direction, including in common humanity, and quite uninteresting as people. Naturally, it flatters them if they and their kind are written up in their own newspapers and those of their friends or rivals, but it is arguable that the only reason they appear is that they are money-men in a society (which includes journalists) that does subconsciously regard money as the new religion, and its manipulators as high priests.

For any youngish individual journalist to attempt to swim against this tide would demand more vision and moral integrity than might reasonably be expected of people who have to earn a living. It is much easier for journalists to play along, and do their best to make money-men sound worthy of notice. They may reason that even if the world becomes a moral and aesthetic pigsty in consequence, the smell may not be too bad in their neighbourhood.

Money as a religion is being supported by journalistic tricks to make it seem nothing of the kind: it is to be seen as 'practical', 'sensible', 'realistic'. Is it in fact any of these things? Few journalists, or any other section of society if they thought about it, would dispute the argument that the world would be a better place if merchant bankers and corporation chief executives were respected rather less and nurses, doctors and creative people more. Not necessarily *paid* more, let us not be Utopian, but respected more as functionaries and human beings.

It is dangerous when society has only one significant yardstick of merit, and doubly so when that yardstick is money. It is still more dangerous when ambitious journalists, whatever their private reservations, use their professional tricks to play by the yardstick and reinforce it rather than challenging it where thought and feeling dictate.

Will this go on for ever, or will there be a change of priorities that is brought about by a change in public mood? We cannot see into the future with certainty, but some journalism is now based on what is a miniature version of such a process.

50

Reporting the Future

Much 'news' coverage today is not news of what has happened, but news of what will or should happen. Reportage has been partly replaced by prediction. In the case of newspapers it may be an attempt to stay ahead of the electronic media in any way possible.

But this sometimes questionable trick is not confined to straightforward and honest prediction of what is likely to happen in the opinion articles and the leader columns of newspapers, and in commentary on radio and television. By extension, it means that embargoes on news releases are hardly ever issued any more because they have been routinely broken to suit the convenience of recipients; and texts of forthcoming speeches, or the gist of them, are regularly leaked to the media in advance, with no embargo, in order to advertise them – and, in the case of a controversial matter, perhaps to soften up the public. So in a sense the journalist is in the prediction business.

Is this trick healthy? On several grounds it is not. The loss of rigid separation between what has happened and what will, maybe, happen has a price. It is that the public is encouraged to think that all coverage of events is just a lot of wall to wall 'media froth' that does not deserve their full attention.

The preliminary to this mood is the familiar irritation. Suppose that a commentator on the radio says at eight in the morning: 'At the Confederation of British Industry annual conference this afternoon, the Minister for Employment will tell employers that they ought to treat their employees better.'

Immediately the listener is tempted to ask: 'Is this chap trying to play God? How does he know what the Minister for Employment is going to say this afternoon?' And the delegates to the CBI conference are very likely to think: 'Now we know in advance what he is going to say, or more or less, is there any point in listening to his speech?'

It may be argued that such premature and predictive statements are only a sort of 'trailer' for the minister's speech such as radio, television or the cinema might run as a bait to a future potential audience. That argument holds good only up to a point. All such entertainment trailers have a 'hook', or intriguing black hole, that is calculated to fascinate and attract the punter.

On the contrary, intimations of future speeches usually follow the journalistic principle of putting the main facts in the intro. This is the equivalent of a trailer for a mystery-thriller feature film that gives away the ending: no film distribution company would be mad enough to screen such a trailer.

If the 'what will happen' trick is bad for the public, leaving life as a blur of actual events and predictions of events, it is also bad for the politicians and public figures whose sayings and doings are subject to such an approach. It enables them to trim and cut their speeches in the light of any public reaction to the prediction, and to tone down any sentiment that has caused resentment, blaming the early reports of their future speech as 'speculation'.

By doing so, of course, they would not make friends in the media. But in practice the risk of permanent rupture is minimal since the media need to be spoon-fed with such leaks of future intentions, and it is not in their interests to be permanently angry at being 'taken for a ride'.

Prophecy as distinct from the reportage of real events is not so much in the interest of the public, or even of politicians and other leaders, as of the media themselves. The news-breaking role previously played by newspapers having been taken over by radio and television, newspapers themselves have been forced into carrying reams of comment and opinion, and into adopting tricks, to be in the vanguard of what can be passed off as a news story – such as a leak, reliable or not, about future intentions.

Radio and television have responded with a trick of their own: having such predictive material in their early morning bulletins before the public has had a chance to receive and look at the newspapers, and in their evening bulletins when evening newspapers have long since printed their final editions.

The result is a bundle of tricks from journalists that is possibly more calculated to impress the public (or themselves) than to give an accurate picture of what has happened in the world, as distinct from what will, or may, happen. The world might in time be reduced to a constant media-babble in which it would be all too easy to lose sight of what is important and what is not; of what has actually happened from what some primed or guessing journalist, or his medium, wants the public to think has happened.

The process may become circular when journalists report not only on future subject matter but also on attempts by various people to 'spin' the subject to their own advantage. This now happens not merely in the media pages but also in the general news columns and feature pages.

51

Distortion and Spin as the Story

In some journalism, increasing liberties may be taken in tampering with the record. A whole series of ways of doing this, which might have been regarded as off-limits halfway through the twentieth century, were far from unknown by the end of it.

This eating away at the truth is achieved in both niggling and bold ways. One of the possible niggling ways is for a sub-editor or editor to introduce into a reporter's story, or feature writer's article, facts or sentiments of his own or from the management which the writer might or might not have wanted to use. In practice, this procedure usually comes to light only when the writer does not agree with the sentiments, and is moreover of sufficient public standing to make a public protest. At lower levels, the journalists are more or less powerless because they are fearful of being separated from their meal-ticket.

Let us suppose that a feature writer composes an article arguing that the Home Secretaries of both main parties have been negligent in not tackling the problems of racial conflict more positively, hoping that eventually they will simply go away. He writes as follows:

> The present Home Secretary is in a difficult position. Racial tension has built up so much in recent years in communities like Bradford and Brixton that a careless word could do much more damage than it would have done twenty years ago, when hostile attitudes among the ethnic groups and the indigenous population were not at present levels of danger.

What appears is this:

> The present Home Secretary is in a more difficult position than his predecessors, largely through his own inactivity. When he was at the Department of Employment his record was no better, indeed it was he who allowed unemployment to rise and unemployment benefits to be cut. With disastrous consequences, he has again allowed his own apathy and weakness in Cabinet to wreck the chances of racial peace in areas like Bradford and Brixton. He now faces a situation in which a careless word could do much more damage than it would have done twenty years ago, when hostile attitudes among the ethnic groups and the indigenous population were not at present levels of danger.

The insertion of the highly prejudicial extra material entirely alters the thrust of the article, which was not in the first place hostile to the Home Secretary personally but which, when augmented, most definitely is. This is a deliberately exaggerated, extreme example, concocted only for the purposes of illustration. The alterations might have been more subtle.

If in such a case the contributor was himself a politician or a figure with a public reputation outside the media, a protest, perhaps a public one, would almost inevitably follow. If he was a staff journalist who was dependent on the goodwill of his boss, or a freelance journalist living in hope of further commissions, a protest – certainly a public one – would be less likely.

As a result, such 'enhancements' of stories and articles, though probably not so spectacular, may be commoner today than they were. Certainly if the writer was a public figure and the insertion or insertions were too radical, we might well hear about it, especially as rivals in the media jungle could enjoy reporting on the matter as a form of soap-opera rather than as a tragedy for the craft of journalism.

One would assume that anyone who performed or sanctioned such changes in a story or article under someone else's by-line would be regarded as grossly unprofessional and be subject to a request that he considered his position. In practice, the perpetrators have sometimes been regarded not as presumptuous buffoons but, at worst, as subjects for amusement.

Other methods of introducing 'spin' have been bolder and more far-reaching. Let us suppose this time that it is the same Home Secretary himself who writes an article for a newspaper on the need for the ethnic population to identify more strongly with the indigenous population, especially in such highly mixed areas as Bradford and Brixton. He expresses the view that ethnic populations should not be entirely wrapped up in their own original culture but should regard themselves as part of the nation in which they have chosen to live.

Such a point would be thought by many people to be no more than common sense, and certainly not racist. But suppose the newspaper that published it puts over it the heading: 'Home Secretary to Blacks: Dump Your Own Culture'.

Suppose also someone there slightly re-writes the first paragraph to give more power to this sentiment rather than to the general drift of the Home Secretary's article. And finally, suppose that the Home Secretary objects, and publicly protests at what he calls the 'spin' that has been put on the article. What would the result be?

The answer is: another story for that newspaper, and for others, too. The *way* stories are treated can now become news. It may be the case that for the general reader, the story is obscure and irritating. But to politicians and the media it will be of unfailing interest; and, since the media sometimes have a shaky notion of what will interest their general readers, apart from beer, sex and fashion, stories about who spun what, and how and why, will now often run and run.

We have been talking about journalistic spin. More importantly, governments and other powerful bodies have their own spin-machines for distorting stories before they are even written. That is the bold way of tampering with the truth. Stories with a particular slant, a particular choice of facts, and a particular choice of facts that are *not* mentioned, are fed to favoured journalists. In itself this is not the journalists' fault; and it is asking too much to expect them simply to decline such stories, whatever their source.

'Spun' stories are tricks that are bound to be attacked by those who hold opposing views. In which case, the spin *as* the story may sometimes be a necessary corrective to distortion. On occasion, there can be a flow of stories about such spinning and its practitioners: a public display of the methods both of the media and of the spinners that can for a time make figures like Alastair Campbell as famous as the people they serve, or even more so.

But the level of interest in what journalists write, and why, is still apt to be much higher among journalists themselves than among those who do not practise the craft. Even denunciations of spin can fall on apathetic ears elsewhere, as can warnings that a bottle may not live up to its label, or that a story may not live up to its heading.

52

Headlines and Fib-lines

The headline or other heading that says just a little bit more than the story itself can support is now a commoner journalistic trick than it was before radio and, especially, television strongly challenged the print media. More than occasionally, you will find that when you search the intro, or have even read the entire story, the claims of the heading will not have been fully sustained. Some fictitious but not uncharacteristic examples of the trick may illustrate the point.

Union Chief Threatens Strike
The leader of the General Purposes Union, Syd Blank, said yesterday that strike action could not be ruled out if the government persisted in granting much less generous pay awards in the public sector than were being paid by private firms.

'We are trying to cooperate with the government in providing better public services,' said Mr Blank. 'We will do everything we can to avoid industrial action, but we have been making our appeal for fairness to the government for several years now, and if the government refuses to take aboard the justice of our claim, industrial action is one of the many future courses we cannot entirely rule out.'

Here the story, from the intro downwards, does not support the heading, although readers with little sense of, or interest in, the precise meaning of words may be deceived by the trick. The most that the trade union leader actually said was that *industrial action* could not be ruled out. Industrial action can have many forms other than strikes. He did not say, 'Strikes will not be ruled out'. He did not mention strikes. His reference was to industrial action. Even less did he 'threaten' strikes.

'Threat' is a bonus word in this deception, because using it may inflame the other side in the dispute and whip up the atmosphere in such a way that more news stories are likely to be produced. This may be satisfactory from the point of view of journalists, but it is not so satisfactory from that of the trade union leader, public employers or the public.

Miracle Cancer Cure Discovered
A possible cure for cancer has been found by researchers in a hospital in the north of England.

'If further tests on mice prove positive, we may just possibly have the means of keeping the condition in remission,' said Dr Josh Hope, leader of the research team. 'It is too early to say whether this will be a cure for cancer, but we believe it could have a considerable impact on the condition, and further research may indicate whether it would be likely to have the same effect on humans.'

Here the heading takes the story several notches beyond anything suggested in it. The doctor has said plainly that it is too early to judge whether this will prove to be a cure for cancer in mice, let alone humans, restricting himself to the truthful but less exciting statement that it could have a 'considerable impact' on cancer.

Nowhere does anyone suggest that a 'cure' for cancer has been found, as is implied by the heading. The story is only about a means of keeping cancer in remission, i.e. dormant and not progressing.

The heading, 'Miracle Cancer Cure Discovered' is therefore either careless or an attempt to 'soup up' one of the dozens of stories about hoped for cures for cancer that appear in the course of any decade.

Model Has 'Slept With 500 Men'
The model and PR party-attender extraordinaire Fifi Flytee boasted yesterday that she had had 500 lovers.

'These stories that I have had 500 lovers have been chasing me since I was eighteen,' she said, 'and I have never bothered to deny them. They are fantastic.'

Miss Flytee, who made headlines when she appeared at a launch party at the Groucho Club wearing only an orange fur hat and Calvin Klein spectacles, said that her first lover had been a page-boy at a Liverpool hotel when she was fourteen. 'He took me out for the evening and we held hands as we overlooked the docks,' she said. 'It was very romantic.'

When her romance with a wealthy Egyptian lawyer broke up, she was nineteen and, she said, 'went completely to pieces' and had taken to going out with every man she could find. '500 is pretty optimistic,' she joked, 'but there were quite a lot.' She denied reports that she was still a virgin, and that her so-called affairs with a broadcaster, a peer and an actor were for publicity purposes only.

In this case, the heading seems to be based less on fact, or admission or boasting, than on the supposition that fashion and PR riff-raff will not sue, however great the provocation, because they are all too aware that they depend on the media for the publicity that is their lifeblood in the absence of any great talent, or indeed any talent at all. The heading seems to rely on the further supposition that any allegation made inside quotation marks doesn't really count. Any journalist who believes that should try, without the benefit of a court hearing or some other endorsement, a heading reading: 'Bishop "Stole Drugs"'.

Nowhere does Miss Flytee say she has slept with 500 men. She says that such stories have been 'chasing her' since she was eighteen, which suggests that she is saying that they are untrue. She adds that she has never bothered to fight them, thus implying that, if she had bothered, she could have truthfully denied them. She then says something that is either accidentally or deliberately ambiguous: that the stories are 'fantastic'. As media-created 'celebrities' are seldom precise in their use of words, this could mean that such stories are 'fanciful', or else that she regards them as 'wonderful'. Either way, they do not add up to a confirmation that she has been physically penetrated by 500 men.

By her reference to the page-boy at the Liverpool hotel, she makes it clear that her definition of a 'lover' does not automatically and necessarily include sexual intercourse, whereas a modern readership would probably assume that it did. When she says that she had a 'romance' with a wealthy lawyer, it could mean a lot or a little. After her acquaintance with him breaks up, she admits to 'going to pieces' and looking around for any man she could find, and she apparently found quite a lot. But even that does not support the '500 lovers' heading.

Miss Flytee probably will not attempt to sue, although she might if that were likely to bring her more publicity. All she will do to support the '500 lovers' heading is to say that there have been 'quite a lot' of lovers, which is a purely subjective and titivating statement rather than a straight denial. Even if she makes no complaint, the reader probably does have a legitimate complaint: that he has been trickily titivated rather than given any facts.

There can, however, be an element of injustice in a blanket condemnation of journalists by the public, especially as it is the public which provides the money that assures the survival of the media. In certain cases journalists' rationalizations of their practices may be regarded as merely glib. But they should not always be so regarded.

53

In Extenuation: Part 1

Journalists are often accused of distorting news values for sensationalist or propaganda purposes, and sometimes they do. The three-quarters of a column on the front page about a pop singer's drug problems together with the three-quarters of an inch on page 19 about an earthquake in Africa leaving several hundred dead is an extreme phenomenon in the media scene, but a familiar one.

But even the most suspicious reader must accept that journalists do not and cannot work to the exact standards that may apply in other important occupations. The early News Extra edition of the London *Evening Standard* on 11 March 2002 ran as its front-page lead story an account of how satellite images had revealed that parts of London were sinking. Subsidence had occurred along the route of the extension to the new Jubilee Underground line and a new tunnel to carry electricity.

The satellite pictures had shown that the affected parts of the capital had sunk by as much as two centimetres in five years. In addition, about twenty-two square miles in south London had sunk by between two and five centimetres in the 1990s, and parts of Mitcham, Tooting and Merton had subsided by about two centimetres between 1996 and 2000.

The story was accompanied by a grim black and white map of the affected areas, showing in jet black the areas of worst subsidence.

By the later, Late Prices Extra, edition, the story of the sinking of London had been relegated to page 4 to make way for a story about an attractive eighteen-year-old British girl who had been killed by a crocodile in Kenya. It appeared alongside a colour picture of the honey-blonde young girl.

There were lots of touching quotes from the girl's uncle, including one on her being 'the most beautiful girl in the world': 'everyone who knew her loved her'.

A cynic might say that the changing of the front-page lead story was typical of the questionable news standards of the day; the sinking of London being ousted by a story about a photogenic girl. After all, the *Evening Standard* is the remaining mainstream evening paper specifically covering London, and what could be more important than the news that parts of the city are sinking? Could a girl's death, even a pretty girl's death, be held to be more important?

In fact the issue, typical of those that editorial executives face from day to day, is not really so clear-cut. Decisions can rarely be based on criteria that are exact and watertight. If one had been present at the editorial conference at which the decision had to be taken, the arguments heard would probably have been on the following lines.

Those who wanted to keep the 'London-is-sinking' story in its front-page lead position would have argued that the paper was the sole remaining mainstream evening paper of the capital and as such was interested in all aspects of the welfare of London; that 'London sinking steadily' was a news story that was of direct interest to millions of people in London itself and to many more millions who habitually visit it; that the misfortunes of one girl and her family could hardly compare with that.

Those who wanted to relegate the story to an inside page in favour of the story about the crocodile victim would have argued that the subsidence of London or anywhere else was a slow-moving running story of little greater urgency today than it would have tomorrow, or the next day; that the crocodile incident was a new story with exotic overtones that were of great human interest; that news is about the unusual, and being mutilated and killed by a crocodile is more unusual than subsidence; that the girl came from Barnet, which made her of local interest; that what had happened to her raised questions about proper supervision that were of social importance and of interest to all parents thinking of sending their children – or allowing their children to go – on adventure holidays; and, finally, that human life and the taking of it must always have priority.

All these points, on both sides, would have been valid. When we consider them, it is easy for us to see that the substitution of the dead girl story for the subsidence story would not merely have been a triumph of a pretty face over an impending disaster that might affect millions.

It may be true that some tabloid newspapers dodge anything that would require an attention span of more than thirty seconds, and largely restrict themselves to tacky misdeeds of trivial 'celebrities' who might not have been heard of among educated people. But such an extreme trick is still by no means universal practice. Even those who practise it tend to leaven it with stronger material: often, in their leading articles and feature articles, tabloid newspapers do express vigorous good sense.

All of which is not the only thing that can be said in extenuation.

54

In Extenuation: Part 2

If some tricks journalists play amount to an offensive, some are an honourable defensive response. They are a defence against the machinations of Authority to conceal the truth from the public. However annoying journalistic tricks may be, the point and value of journalism remains precisely this: that it can tell the people the truth however much Authority would prefer to keep it dark.

Much officially – or organizationally – released compromising information today goes out on the internet, often in such a tedious statistical form that the journalist could almost be excused for losing heart before he has ploughed through half of it, and for failing to see the contentious issue the organization is trying to conceal or play down. The institution releasing the information – ministry, company or other organization – can claim to have made the information public. What more could it have been expected to do?

At the same time, can the journalist who does sift right through the facts and figures on the internet be blamed for exacting revenge on a body that has obliquely tried to hoodwink him? Can he be blamed if he concentrates on the most compromising fact or statistic he discovers, and writes his story from that angle, however unrepresentative it may be of the whole?

Journalists are often cultivated by 'sources' in the hope that they will more readily succumb to 'spin' on any story, or that they will be more ready to write favourable stories based on revealed facts. Isn't it natural that the journalist will occasionally rebel against being used in this way, and prove his independence by giving his source a few knocks?

Those issuing information to journalists are becoming expertly manipulative in the way they do it. There was outrage when, on the day of the destruction of the twin towers of the World Trade Center in New York, an official of a British government department told her staff that that day would be a good one to issue news that they wanted buried as far as possible, since the world would be too concerned with New York to notice.

Some of the resulting moral indignation was a little over-played: this lady had only put onto paper or into the computer facts on the politic presentation of news that those in her department must have known about already. Of course, officials choose the 'good' times, the times when no one is noticing very much, to release unpalatable facts. The time can be 'good' because a big news story is distracting people's attention, or because it is a moment when media people are thinking about other things, including golfing weekends.

The Friday night syndrome is an anti-journalist trick about which journalists have to be constantly on their guard, matching their tricks to the tricks of those issuing unpalatable facts. Five or six pm on a Friday is a very good time for such releases. Journalists, anxious to get away for the weekend, will tend to do a brief story and then depart for the open air. What else can they be expected to do? If it is a political story, they know that on Friday MPs will be travelling to their constituencies and, even in the era of the mobile phone, may not be easy to pin down for comments that would lengthen the story and thus make it more conspicuous.

There is a further benefit for those who release news late on a Friday. The news will appear in Saturday's newspapers, and Saturday's newspapers are assumed to be read as pure entertainment: for the TV and show listings and the frothy interviews with 'stars' rather than for hard news. So a story released to newspapers late on a Friday may not only lead to a scamped story but also – or so the spinners will reason to themselves – a story which is not paid much attention to by the readers of Saturday's newspapers.

Can one blame diligent journalists if they say to themselves, 'We are being mucked about!' and in response contrive the least tolerant interpretation they can of the facts being slithered out so inconspicuously, even if they have to ruin their social Friday evening? The temptation to give undue prominence to something someone wants kept hidden is almost universal among journalists. It amounts to a battle of wills, a game with its own arcane rules, which are more important than mere tricks.

So a daily newspaper journalist who on Friday night has done a brief story on a subject the spinners would like buried, may well be tempted to return to the same subject on Sunday night for Monday's newspaper, following it up after seeing what the Sunday newspapers have done with it, and developing further all the angles the spinners would wish the public not to think about.

Some 'destructive' journalism consists of exactly that. The 'obsessiveness' of such stories, and such campaigns, might not have reached those extremes if there had not in the first place been an attempt to put the journalist at a disadvantage in trying to produce a coherent story.

Sunday newspapers are to a certain extent well placed to exploit Friday evening announcements, except that at the weekend they may not be able to get hold of people who might help develop and lengthen a story. It is quite likely that, as we have seen, recognizing the trick being played on them, journalists will play their own trick back, by not only writing a hostile interpretation of the facts for Monday morning's newspapers but also by further blackening the source by accusing it of that contemporary disease, 'spin-doctoring': manipulating the release of news to suit a hidden purpose.

In these and related ways, journalists who play tricks may only be taking counter-measures against tricks being played on them. Any plea for more 'responsible' journalism would have to be accompanied by a plea for more responsible methods of managing and releasing news.

Will either side budge? To resort to three clichés for the price of one: watch this space, but don't hold your breath.

One of the other difficulties is that downright lies can be told by people who, in the eyes of the public, may be seen as being far above that sort of thing.

55

In Extenuation: Part 3

Even people who are suspiciously watchful of journalists would have to concede that they are sometimes, perhaps often, sinned against rather than sinning, and that their misdoings are frequently triggered by the tactics of those they are reporting on or dealing with.

Lying to journalists, or deceiving them without uttering a factual untruth, can appear to be a competitive sport in areas of politics and commerce – and sometimes in other areas where it might be assumed that integrity should be taken for granted. One of my first unpleasant experiences of this phenomenon was in the world of over fifty years ago, when lying to newspapers, or to anyone else for that matter, was thought to be rather infra dig as well as dangerous.

As a local newspaper reporter, I interviewed a local headmaster, face to face in his office, about a controversial dispute affecting his school. I telephoned him later to check some points and wrote a completely accurate report. After its publication, the headmaster complained to the editor that I had never interviewed him, and so must have made up the story and faked any notes I had. He was a responsible local citizen and an experienced professional; I was a very young and inexperienced reporter. Fortunately the editor's view of me was that I was not a person who would be likely do such a thing, which would have involved crass stupidity as well as dishonesty, since any such invention would inevitably have rebounded heavily on me. Also, another member of the staff had happened to listen in to my telephone conversation with the headmaster on another earpiece, and was able to say that it definitely confirmed that a face-to-face interview had taken place.

I have never automatically taken 'respectable' people at face value ever since. Even 'respectable' people can lie when the results of a story for which they have been interviewed prove to be inconvenient to them. Even if they are not naive, reckless or dishonest enough to say that an interview never took place, they may say that they never made a remark that is attributed to them – and the modern swing away from shorthand note-taking in favour of electronic devices that can be switched off and on and be generally temperamental, makes such an accusation more difficult to resist. They may say that the journalist has breached an understanding about the terms on which the interview would be conducted.

The contemporary ethos, in which some politicians have clearly taken the view that 'the truth' is simply what they can impose on the public mind by media manipulation and other means at any particular moment, has inflamed this tendency.

But it would be lethal to the fabric of society if, because of mutual misbehaviour and mutual counter-attacks, it came about that neither politicians nor journalists were believed about *anything*. Regrettably, there are intimations that this may have happened already. One of them is the inclusion of journalists as well as politicians in the vox-pop lists of the people who win public respect and esteem least.

The hard truth is that some journalistic tricks are justified as the only means by which vital information can be unearthed. If a journalist soft-soaps a clever fraudster by posing as a possible future victim, that trick might be considered by fair-minded people to be justified. If a journalist takes a job in an hotel in order to investigate the exploitation of foreign workers, that trick might be considered by fair-minded people to be justified. And if he poses as a political extremist in order to penetrate a dangerously violent cell, that trick might also be considered to be justified.

A measure of deceit may be involved in such cases, but only people who insist on an impossible degree of purity would be likely to regard it as unjustified. The world can be a rough place, and the techniques of journalism must sometimes be correspondingly rough. The test of any journalistic trick must surely be that it serves the public good, not merely public voyeurism, prurience or envy of successful people.

Of any group of stories, it may be sensible to ask which falls into which category. Some simple but, I hope, possibly useful questions may be asked by anyone who finds that a story makes him uneasy.

56

Relevant Questions

Here are some questions it may pay the reader, listener or viewer to ask himself about pieces of journalism, many of which will pass the test:

1. Is it true? What evidence is given in support of an assertion or allegation?
2. Does it matter? Do the stated facts warrant a conclusion of any importance?
3. Is the illusion of malpractice on the part of someone or some body being unfairly enhanced by the use of prejudicial words?
4. Is a report on someone's actions and comments the result of spontaneous observation or of provocation through angled questioning that effectively puts words in a person's mouth?
5. Does some on-the-spot reporting derive from the un-influenced observations of the reporter, or from 'the view (probably a well known one) back in the office'? What is your hunch?
6. If unidentified 'friends' are quoted in a story about a person, what are the chances of the friends being genuine or of them being conveniently made up?
7. Are reported demands for apologies merely a ritual pre-liminary in the quest for blood?
8. Is it really a scandal, or just an attempt to create one?
9. Can critics be human beings? Consider the unique pressures on them. Would you, after seeing an impressive land-scape, or making love, like being compelled to write an immediate 600 words about it?
10. Is a person's reported conduct as deplorable as it is im-plied, or is the suggestion in the report based on the yob's perspective? Is, for instance, the fact that the Queen or the Prime Minister has to use more expensive transport than you and me simply what you would expect of people with

jobs that are highly important for the rest of us, or is it only a scandal when viewed from the yob's perspective?

11. Does what is being written up, or talked up as a point of principle, really involve a point of principle?

12. Do the inferences being drawn from a press photograph of a person or a scene stand up, or does the picture contradict the text?

13. Is there such a thing as a broadsheet as distinct from a tabloid newspaper any more?

14. What responsibility do journalists bear for contemporary money worship?

15. Has something actually happened, or has someone merely predicted that something is going to happen; or previewed a yet-to-be-delivered speech, or floated an idea?

16. Is what you are reading or hearing a real news story, or only 'spin' – or even just the media and the politicians analysing and commenting on alleged media 'spin'?

17. Partly on the strength of the past form of the individual journalist, and partly on the strength of your own intuitive judgment, do you finally trust the journalist who is involved, or not? And even if you do, do you trust his employers?

In Conclusion

It is an old truism that honesty is the best policy. That doesn't mean that honesty would be wonderful and lovely if only we could afford it. The point is essentially a practical one: that honesty is on the whole likely to be a more effective and lasting policy than crookery because it is more difficult to shoot down; that honesty can be pursued deliberately as a profitable policy, even by someone with enough intelligence and imagination to be capable of thinking up clever, or clever-clever, tricks to deceive people.

That is all very well if you believe in tomorrow. It may well be true, in an unstable society and an internally and externally challenged civilization like our own, in which all sorts of people own newspapers, and television stations are bought and sold like commodities, that there is a temptation to get away with as much as possible in the general turbulence and panic, and to think no further than how to make the fastest and biggest buck in both the literal and figurative senses.

Is this process inevitable, or can it be changed? It is ironic that, in the USA, the originator of 'yellow journalism', where television presents as great a challenge to the press as it does in Britain, much newspaper journalism is now more soberly to the point than the British version. On the front page of one *New York Times* digest that formed part of *The Sunday Telegraph* of 18 June 2006, chosen at random, there were three major stories.

They were 'China's Black Cloud Casts a Global Shadow', describing in unforced presentation and language the environmental costs of the Chinese industrial boom; 'From a Former Next President, Warnings of a Warming World', similarly setting out Al Gore's campaign to stimulate action on global-warming remedies; and, in a lighter vein, 'Discriminating Canine Noses Find Gold in Bedbugs and DVDs', the story of how dogs can be hired out to hotels after being trained to detect bedbugs.

Neither in the headings nor in the text of these three examples, or of other stories in the same digest, was there any suggestion of the agitatedly clever-clever, the scatter-gun snide, the deployment of sexual innuendo as a means of attracting the attention of readers who are perceived to be brain-dead, the slyly apocalyptic, or playing to mean-spirited envy and malice.

It *can* be done. So much for the blanket sneers at American journalism for not being as 'professional' as the contemporary British variety. Professional? In the light of some present-day journalism, the question sometimes needs to be asked: what profession exactly?

Certainly, journalists cannot logically plead that the way the age of electronic marvels impinges on their jobs renders 'old fashioned' niceties in the way they do them of no more than secondary importance. In his London *Evening Standard* column of 28 June 2006, the newspaperman Professor Roy

Greenslade of the City University of London argued shrewdly that journalists should keep their nerve in the 'crazy revolutionary race' in technology, and not allow it to divert them from their central task, which was journalism itself. 'The journalism must come first,' he said.

Quite. I would go further: quality journalism is quality journalism, and tricks are tricks, whatever the modernity and complexity of their delivery. Is it naive to believe that journalists should be correctors rather than creators of a partly unconscious mind-set that is bent on getting away with as much as possible, just as some other professionals try to get away with as much as possible, before the roof of our civilization falls in?

Individual journalists should not be blamed without reference to their employers. Good journalism, especially if it involves more than superficial research, takes time, and time costs money. One provincial newspaper group is reported to expect a return of thirty per cent for its investors. Even some industry money-men might regard this as a questionable ambition when newspapers can – and do – thrive on a fraction of this. Are newspaper proprietors in general now little more than cat's-paws for professionally avaricious investors, including banks who are professionally blind to everything except their percentage? How can the best journalism be achieved by strong editorial teams when the emphasis is on editorial cost-cutting – because the editorial side does not of course *directly* produce money – and the bumping up of advertising revenues?

It is easy, in such circumstances, to forget that good journalism is the reason people buy newspapers in the first place. It will be interesting to see whether newspaper readership in general continues to decline, and what explanation the thirty-percenters and their counterparts and rivals will offer for this.

The alternative to a voluntary change in journalistic tricks and journalistic standards could well, on an unwelcome day, be the nightmare of statutory control, that tool of political oppression. Such a development would have been inconceivable fifty years ago except in time of war, but it would not be inconceivable now if there were *support* from a disaffected public.

Even highly regarded and intellectually respectable people

can be in favour of state control of the media, if the occasion seems right. In its *Declaration on the Media* of 1978, UNESCO proposed giving more power to Third World governments to censor information, presumably because it was thought that some information could be destructively inflammatory. The suggestion was dismissed as 'clumsy and impractical' by Professor Paul Kennedy of Yale in his *The Parliament of Man: The United Nations and the Quest for World Government*, published in Britain in 2006.

Would a British government automatically reject such a move because it was thought in some quarters to be 'clumsy and impractical' – if the occasion seemed to be right? As so many provincial and national British newspapers and so much of British television is now in the hands of overseas interests, might a future government more easily consider the moment had come for some state control of the media – perhaps as a way of pandering not only to British distrust of journalists but also to British nationalistic feeling?

Governments can and do work in overt or underhand ways against news organizations if they think there are powerful enough reasons for doing so and they think they can get away with it because the public doesn't much care. In the 1980s, the time of the Conservative government of Mrs Margaret Thatcher, I was covering media stories for *The Guardian* with the media editor Peter Fiddick, and saw how governments can operate when, rightly or wrongly, they don't like the way the news is handled.

In April 1986, the government allowed American aircraft attacking Libya to fly from British bases. Obviously both the BBC and ITV gave a great deal of coverage to Britain's move and to the possible international repercussions, and the BBC came under almost immediate attack from Conservatives for allegedly slanting their news bulletins against Mrs Thatcher. On 29 October, the BBC reported that it had completed its internal inquiry, which saw nothing seriously wrong, and the day after that Norman Tebbit submitted a comparative analysis of the way the BBC and ITV had composed their headlines for their stories, with some sixty or seventy examples, which I read through conscientiously, afterwards facetiously claiming that

I must have been the only journalist in Fleet Street to have done more than read the press summary.

Norman Tebbit was for the political left a devil figure who was bound to be wrong whatever he said. He was accused of 'playing politics'. Of course he was playing politics: he was a politician. But that begged the question of whether what he was saying on this particular occasion was right or not. It must have been obvious, even to lifelong supporters of the BBC like myself, that in this case the BBC had often given an inflection to its headlines that could fairly be summarized as, 'What has this ghastly woman done now, and what horrors are we going to experience by way of retaliation?' Even those who agreed with this sentiment could hardly escape the fact that the BBC, as a public-service broadcaster dependent on public payment of the licence fee, was supposed to be politically impartial: it could report political opinions but it could not display any of its own. By comparison, ITV headlines had been phrased in an uninflected, neutral way. For a BBC supporter, the side-by-side BBC and ITV headings made embarrassing reading.

The BBC brushed it off, to enormous cheering in many sections of the media. I saw that at the time as dangerous hubris and a grave tactical mistake. It left Mrs Thatcher with two alternatives. She could say, 'Well, I suppose we will in future just have to take whatever the BBC throws at us.' Or else she could say, 'We will pound the BBC into rubble.' With her combative nature, which would she choose? Of course.

Things became very uncomfortable for the BBC from that time. Just after the BBC coverage of the Libya issue, a new BBC chairman who was thought to be closer to the establishment than to newsmen was imposed, Marmaduke Hussey. Subsequently a chairman was imported from past service at ITV's London Weekend Television, Christopher Bland. Commercial television companies were favoured at the expense of the BBC wherever possible.

It is true that the government had power over the BBC in a way it did not have over other sectors of the news trade, and the BBC was never allowed to forget that its licence fee, the proceeds of which gave it the freedom to make quality as distinct from populist programmes if it chose, was always a matter for discussion and never to be taken for granted. It was a dire, if oblique, threat. But governments can discover or create powers over practically anything if the will is there and the electoral risk seems to them to be the lesser of two evils. To a government minister who claimed, 'There is no possible way of controlling the media,' the 'right' Prime Minister might reply: 'Find one.' In the future there may be no shortage of pretexts, including the needs of security.

The worst conceivable disaster would be if an authoritarian government that wanted to control journalists and the media through laws suited to its own needs and purposes, was able to do it because the public – supposedly the people the media are there to befriend and protect from unjust government – supported the *government* in its controlling ambitions rather than supporting the *journalists* who are supposed to be there to protect them.

The problem of how to avoid that dire possibility can be solved only through perhaps sometimes painful self-appraisal by journalists – the professionals I have worked with and generally respected and liked for over half a century. We need to regain an awareness of the essential basics of the job in contrast to the 'clever actory' makeup of much of its contemporary public face. The honest rather than tricksy presence of journalists continues to be absolutely vital to individual freedom and to the health of society as a whole.

We can but hope that self-appraisal by journalists, and informed appraisal by the public, will not be too late.

Index

INDEX